Kids love reading
Choose Your Own Adventure®!

Watch for these titles coming up in the
Choose Your Own Adventure® series.

Ask your bookseller for books you have missed
or visit us at cyoa.com to learn more.

CHOOSE YOUR OWN ADVENTURE® 31

TRACK STAR

BY R.A. MONTGOMERY

ILLUSTRATED BY WES LOUIE

CHOOSECO®
WAITSFIELD, VERMONT

Track Star © 2009 Chooseco LLC,
Waitsfield, Vermont. All Rights Reserved.

Cover artwork © 2009 Chooseco LLC,
Waitsfield, Vermont. All Rights Reserved.

Illustrated by: Wes Louie
Book design: Stacey Boyd, Big Eyedea Visual Design

For information regarding permission, write to:

CHOOSECO

P.O. Box 46
Waitsfield, Vermont 05673
www.cyoa.com

ISBN-13: 978-1-933390-31-X
ISBN-10: 1-933390-31-4

Published simultaneously in the United States and Canada

Printed in the United States

0 9 8 7 6 5 4 3 2 1

WORLD
ANTI-DOPING
AGENCY
play true

Produced in cooperation with
the World Anti-Doping Agency.

WWW.WADA-AMA.ORG

To Ramsey

BEWARE and WARNING!

This book is different from other books.

You and YOU ALONE are in charge of what happens in this story.

There are dangers, choices, adventures, and consequences. You must use all of your numerous talents and much of your enormous intelligence. The wrong decision could end in disaster—even death. But, don't despair. At any time, you can go back and make another choice, alter the path of your story, and change its result.

You are a talented student athlete. Your sport is track where you excel in the middle distance events. College has never seemed like an option because of your family's finances, although you've worked very hard your whole life. An athletic scholarship would change your world, but you are surrounded by powerful people and confusing decisions. Not everyone has your best interests at heart. Where does your story lead to next? The decision is up to *you*.

You are a speed demon, and close to being a world-class athlete. The 60, the 100, and the 200 meter relays are your events. You beat almost everybody in your local, regional, and state championships, except Gail Forbes. Forbes is just a fraction of a second ahead of you in most races. Oh, yeah, and don't forget Antonio Helios, another threat and gaining on you.

Next year is your senior year in high school. College scholarships and even sponsorships are up for grabs. This is the big time: your parents can't afford college. So it's now or never.

Lately there have been rumors that your rivals—maybe even Gail—are doping with steroids and other performance-enhancing drugs. Strength, endurance, power all increased by using these substances. Or so they say.

With the huge health issues connected with these substances, is it worth it? You hear that these issues can be as simple as overly large muscles leading to torn tendons, strained ligaments, and sprains. But they can also lead to depression, suicide, or even heart problems later in life—like by age thirty! Thirty seems like a long way away, but it's not.

It's not only the health issues. You could lose your right to race for at least two years if you are found positive for using a banned substance in a doping test. Performance-enhancing substances are banned all over the world by WADA (the World Anti-Doping Agency). Even chess players are banned from using things that kids with ADD use to help them concentrate.

Turn to page 2.

2

Think of stories of athletes who have tested positive. Ruined careers. Lost hopes. Failure, and even jail sentences. Some athletes have even died!

You have heard that coaches sometimes convince kids to try these kinds of things, because it reflects well on the coach to have a winner on the team. You are suspicious of the assistant coach, Samson. He hung around after practice last week. You like the coach. Samson was once a star himself, but his career ended with two torn Achilles tendons. Even when his injury was better, he never ran well again.

"Hey, you're really doing well. But I noticed you running out of steam in the 200 meter. You okay?" he asks, handing you a nut and fruit energy bar—just the kind you like.

"I guess so. It's a tough race," you reply. Both Gail and Helios beat you last week. Not by much, but third is not first—or second.

"What's your diet like?" Samson asks.

"Oh, the regular stuff that the team recommends. Carbs—mostly pasta—the day before the race, and the rest of the time fruit, veggies, protein, lots of water—no cow products. Oh yeah, vitamins."

"Want me to review your food diary? You keep one, don't you? Maybe I can pick out what you need more of or less of. You should be winning. You might even want to change your event; maybe the 400 would suit you."

Go on to the next page.

You know that Samson has worked with many athletes who are surrounded by doping suspicions, including Gail Forbes. So, you ask yourself, *was that a subtle approach to doping or steroids?*

If you pursue this with Samson, turn to page 4. You don't have to agree to drugs, if he offers them.

Gail has been very friendly lately. If you decide to talk with Gail Forbes and bring up the subject of doping, turn to page 9.

If you toy with the idea of asking Antonio Helios what he thinks, turn to page 12.

4

The idea of talking to Samson about doping throws you off. Even your mom notices.

"So long," you say the next morning. "I'll be late getting home. Big practice today. Three days from the All-State Meet."

"You okay, honey? You sound a bit off," she replies.

Your mom is your best friend and she reads you like an open book, but she doesn't crowd you. She respects you. Your dad is a different story: no friendship there.

"Yeah sure, Mom. I'm fine, just nervous about the race and school and stuff like that."

"Okay, just checking. Remember, you can always count on me—no matter what."

A quick hug and you are out the door. It's early, light just sneaking over the low hills surrounding your town. It's not much of a town, mostly old mills that went out of business and converted into expensive condominiums for the engineers, programmers, and lawyers who work in the nearby science park. Lots of fancy cars, gourmet food stores, and health clubs. You have a job on the maintenance crew for two of the condos. It pays fairly well and it's good physical work. You don't mind it. Your bank account is growing.

Usually your long walk stretches your muscles and clears your head. But not today...

Turn to page 6.

"I'll see if I can make some time this summer," you tell Antonio. He just shrugs, smiles, and gives you a nod. Your friendship turns a corner that day. Antonio becomes the one person you can talk to about anything. He shares your views, you think. You are glad you have decided to focus for now, to concentrate on studies and track. Studies come easily, so most of the extra time is on track.

Your half-friendship with Gail dwindles, and you see less and less of him on the track field and almost never in classes. That's the way friendships go, you figure. Here today, gone tomorrow. Anyway, Gail lives in a different world, and the dark rumors swirl about his doping and the crowd he hangs out with. Yet, he does very well in his sprints.

Antonio is doing really well in track, too. The two of you train together and experiment with diet and nutrition, reading up on different food groups, trying different carbo-loading approaches the night before races, and hydrating as much as possible. You establish your own monitoring program based on the protocols you research on the internet. There is a lot of info on the net from WADA, the IOC, UNESCO, the various athletic organizations, and drug and pharmaceutical companies.

Turn to page 61.

First is the constant worry about getting enough financial support for college—scholarships, loans, whatever. Your father had run a small automotive garage, but he had trouble with his partner and went bankrupt. This hangs like a storm cloud over him and the family. He has made it abundantly clear that once out of high school you are on your own. No money. No help. So academics and sports are the only way to get to college.

A high-pitched whine interrupts your thoughts as you take the long familiar walk to school. Looking up to the sky you see a silvery private jet screaming into the light cloud cover. You and that jet are on the same schedule every morning as you make the long walk to school (part of your training regimen).

Who is that person, and where are they going every morning and why? What's their life like? You aren't sure whether or not you envy them. Is it all about power and money? Nothing more?

It doesn't take long before the sound is just a memory, a momentary disturbance in the laminar flow of air in that vast liquid blanket that wraps itself around Earth.

You are jolted back to your own reality by a car filled with kids headed to school. They blast the horn and wave. You know some of them. They're okay, but you don't look up to them as you do good athletes or good students. Some say they have too much money for their own good. You think they respect you because of your track victories. You go your own way.

Turn to page 8.

8

The other thing on your mind is a big choice, something that will affect your entire future. *Is this the beginning of adulthood?* you ask yourself. Is this when it's no longer just fun and games; it's for real. It's for life. Or it could be.

The choice staring you in the face with a grin (or is it a sneer?) is this: do you do anything to win races, including doping or drugs?

On one hand you know the answer—Never! But...maybe, just maybe, there is a middle ground, a ground that can help you and not be risky. Not everything is black or white, is it? There must be legal supplements that can help performance. Didn't that famous Italian ski racer years ago power down six or seven cups of espresso before a race to give himself a burst of energy and concentration? Nothing wrong with coffee. Or is there?

Big things are coming your way, like living on your own, choosing a career, falling in love, maybe even dealing with the death of parents or friends. A kid in the senior class died last year from some weird kind of cancer.

So, what does coach Samson have on his mind? Is his interest in you for the reflected glory of coaching a winner?

Turn to page 14.

Gail Forbes is one of the Golden People at school. You have always admired him from afar. You know the kind—good looks, good grades, popular with girls and guys, great athlete, and: rich. He has everything going for him. *So why would he like me?* you ask yourself.

Maybe because you don't suck up to him. You are a loner, respected as a good athlete and an excellent student, not a geek, but you go your own way. Nobody really knows you. You don't belong to any group. And you like it that way.

Although you keep to yourself, you still have friends, but not very close ones. You miss the opportunity to dig deep and discuss what is getting to you. Right now you are doing really well in track, and your college education might depend on it. Then there's your family and particularly your dad. That's a mess.

Using something to get some extra help on the track would take off some of the pressure. But that is a big decision to make. There really isn't anyone at home to talk to about this; it might be tricky or even dangerous to bring it up with kids you don't really know well. There is Gail, and there are rumors that he uses performance-enhancing substances (why can't they just call them drugs?). Maybe friendship with him would be like a moth getting too close to a flame. Risking all has a flavor to it, a good flavor sometimes, like in a tight race. But risking too much can turn sour. Really sour.

Turn to the next page.

The next day after practice, you approach him.

"Hey, Gail, got a minute?"

"Sure, what's up?" he replies. You can't help but like him.

"Well, you see, I mean...."

"Spit it out! I don't bite." He laughs, but it is a friendly laugh not meant to torment or demean.

"Doping. Drugs. Steroids, stuff like that," you say in a muted tone.

"Wowzer," Gail replies, not looking at you. "Well, how about coming over to my house. Too hot to discuss here."

"Great. When?" you ask.

"Right now." He moves off toward the parking lot and his car. You follow.

The school parking lot is usually crowded, and today is no exception. You wonder where these kids get the money to buy a car. Even more than that, how do they manage to run them: gas, tires, repairs, insurance, all that stuff. You don't waste any time thinking about a car, no way. That's out of reach for you.

Gail's car is a dream beyond dreaming for you, an apple red foreign sports car. You have never even seen one like it except for Gail's. Its cost would be enough for a family of four to live a whole year or more. Gail's world seems more like a dream than reality.

Go on to the next page.

"Hey Gail, wuz up?" yells a star linebacker on the football team from across the parking lot. There are several other football players with him just getting into a late model SUV. Everyone likes Gail.

"Same, same, dudes," Gail yells back waving and smiling.

The car smells of new leather and you can't help but feel envy slipping in. Pulling out of the car park several more kids yell greetings and wave; you feel a sense of pride just being in the car with Gail. You don't like the feeling. You are not Gail. You are you, just you.

Home for Gail is a McMansion on the east side of town. This is where the doctors, lawyers, financial people, and other high net-worth types live. Their huge, ugly houses are lined up like matching cereal boxes. Expensive cars sit in big driveways. Lately there are more and more 'For Sale' signs sprouting up outside. *Greed can destroy, there is no question about that,* you say to yourself. You wonder if Gail's parents are ever affected by the economy.

Turn to page 18.

Antonio Helios could become your best friend, you think. You'd like that. He is bright, hard working, and has a great family: three younger brothers, an older sister, and twin sisters still in diapers. They are from Guatemala. Antonio's dad works for a carpet cleaning company and their mom takes care of the kids. They have been in the US for about five years—Antonio is sketchy about when they arrived and you have wondered if they are citizens. You like the whole family and spend a lot of time with them. Poor as they might be, and with all those mouths to feed, you always have a place at their table. And boy is the food good: chicken, beans, chilies, rice, soup, tortillas with tomato salsa. You envy Antonio.

You judge that you can bring anything up with Antonio and it would be like putting it in a safe. He does not gossip, of this you are sure. The whole subject of doping or using performance-enhancing substances—drugs—to help you win is bothersome. It's real, it's out there, kids do use them (and kids and top athletes do get caught and end up in deep trouble with the law and with their athletic associations).

So, you decide to bring the whole subject up with Antonio. He has the same problem that you have: big dreams and talent, but no money for college.

Go on to the next page.

Antonio invites you over to his *casa* Tuesday after practice. Now could be the time to bring it up. This is worrisome stuff.

Sure enough, you are invited to stay for dinner. It's pepian, a thick meat and vegetable stew, and of course frijoles (black beans cooked and mashed). Spicy chilies are always on hand. You love spicy food, which you rarely (like never—your dad hates it) get at home. Often you bring a gift like sweets for the kids or fresh baked bread that your mom makes once a week.

The house is small, the whole family crowded into four rooms; but it is always fun and full of laughter, except when the twins are crying. After dinner you and Antonio go outside and sit in chairs around a small table under a peach tree. Antonio's parents and most of the kids are watching a game show on TV.

"Antonio, I want to talk—" you begin.

"About doping," he says.

You are stunned—he read your mind. You always knew that Antonio was gifted—look at him in math, a wizard—but now you realize that he is wise beyond his years.

"You know? Don't you? I mean about doping and drugs and stuff?" you say.

"Of course. I live in the real world. I see everything in this world, not very nice things. Drugs are a part of this world." He turns to the surrounding small houses and buildings. "See this area. It is a barrio not as bad as it was in my old town in Guatemala, but bad nonetheless. Lives are ruined by drugs. So, my friend, what is it you want to know?"

Turn to page 26.

14

You have trouble paying attention in class. You're worried about your future. The image of that jet plane you see every morning haunts you. What would he or she do? And what did they do to get where they are?

Finally the last bell of the day clangs. You are free to go to practice—and to see Coach Samson. But you don't feel very free.

Samson glances at you from across the field but turns his attention to three hurdlers. They are all pretty good. It's a tough race, those hurdles. You are glad you don't do them. Is Samson ignoring you? You feel as though the whole world is watching you and listening in on your thoughts.

If you decide to approach Samson directly,
turn to page 15.

If you let it slide, letting fate make your decision,
turn to page 67.

The oval inside the 400 meter track is where the field event people practice. Shot put, discus, even javelin athletes train in the oval. Long jump, high jump, and pole vault are in the field next to the track. It is a busy world, a world unto itself. Even though these are high school students, they all take their event with the seriousness of high level athletes. You like being part of this incredible world of track and field—dating back some five thousand years to the ancient games that eventually lead to the Olympics. You are proud and frightened at the same time.

Now it's time to talk with Samson. But what should you say? Should you be up front and bring up doping or drugging or whatever they call it these days? Or, do you just play it cool and talk about doing a food diary and getting on a better training schedule? Maybe you should just forget the whole thing. There he is standing alone as if he were waiting for just you.

Out of the corner of your eye, you spot Gail finishing a sprint, walking off the adrenaline rush from pushing the limits. Gail is your closest friend on the team, but do you trust Gail—really trust him? It's all too confusing. Being adult is no easy job, maybe that's why so many fail at it.

Turn to page 17.

"Watch out!" someone yells, panic in his voice.

A javelin soars through the air, its trajectory thrown off by the thrower's misstep. It closes with the ground fast and slices into the turf, quivering as it buries its metal point. No one is hurt, but the lesson is clear: be alert, this isn't a sand box.

You try to be nonchalant about the whole thing, but you are shaken. Peering around, you check to be sure that no other javelin or discus is headed your way.

Now Samson is nowhere to be seen. Where did he go? Is this some kind of game he is playing with you? Should you track him down at his office or even his house? Or should you ask some of the other kids about him (being careful not to reveal too much if you do). Some kids believe that doping is just part of the process of becoming the best— no big deal. Others would turn you in if they thought you were a doper. On the other hand, many kids just don't care about other people's choices. What's it to them?

The wind is picking up, and you're a bit chilly from your workout. You put on a hooded sweatshirt trying to decide your next move.

If you ask questions of some of the kids, like the three hurdlers, turn to page 30.

If you decide to search Coach Samson down turn to page 33.

18

"So, here's the crib. Like it?" Gail asks, getting out of the car.

The house is a three-story Victorian-style mess with towers and porches and high windows and brick work and stone work and lots of chimneys. Impressive but ugly, built to make a statement but not balanced or done with a sense of proportion or aesthetics.

"Great," is all you can muster in reply. Your own house is a two bedroom bungalow not much bigger than Gail's parents' four-car garage.

Gail leads the way into the house; no one is home except for the cook. She isn't particularly welcoming.

Gail leads the way to a large room complete with huge plasma TV, shelves loaded with DVDs, an entertainment center, two giant couches, easy chairs, and refrigerator and stove top.

"This is where I hang," Gail says, spreading his hands to enclose the space. You are struck with how impersonal it is. There is nothing of Gail in it, just expensive stuff, and lots of it.

"Okay, here's the deal. If you are serious about doping, then you're in right now. There's a vow of silence you have to take. We don't kid around. If it's not for you, that's okay, we'll hang for a while, no problem, you are always welcome, but no more talk about this subject. Got it?"

If you decide to "be in" and take the vow, turn to page 40.

If you decide to opt out, turn to page 20.

20

The whole thing smells like dead fish to you. It's one thing to envy someone like Gail; it's a different thing to try and BE Gail and take on his lifestyle. You follow your gut and the gut says NO, NO, NO!

Gail doesn't like it one bit that you want out. You see the color rising in his face to bright crimson, his nostrils flaring, and his blue eyes closing and getting hard looking.

"Beat it, you wuss! If I ever hear of you talking about this you will be history, big time. Get my meaning?" He stalks about the room like some predatory beast who has just lost his prey.

Go on to the next page.

Time to make tracks, you say to yourself.

"Sure, sure. You can count on it. Lips are sealed. Anyway, what talk? As far as I'm concerned we never had any talk." You finish up by heading for the door.

Now you are down the corridor out the door, free and into fresh, clean air.

But you have no car. You came with Gail and you don't know this part of town. There aren't any bus stops here in McMansion-land. You'll have to hoof it. So, get to it.

Turn to page 22.

Days pass with nights filled with nightmare dreams about gangs and beatings and worse. You skip practice for two days and when you do go back you vary your hours so as not to run into to Gail. You feel as though you are not real, as though you are but a shadow. Your coaches notice it and one in particular, Coach Bud Devlin, asks you to a meeting. You don't know him well but he is likable and a great coach, despite being one of the youngest ones ever.

Bud takes you to a diner near your school famous for its veggie burgers, smoothies, and oven-baked vegetable fries. You take a booth at the back, away from the kids who are hunched over iPods, Blackberries, and iPhones. They seem so wrapped up in their electronic worlds that they probably wouldn't listen in anyway.

"What's up? Problems at home? Love problems? Money?" he asks in a frontal attack. At least he doesn't play games.

"None of the above," you reply. You are now on slippery ground. Should you trust him or not? If you do, just how much trust? Boy, do you feel lonely. A friend is just what you need.

Bud toys with a straw in his smoothie—banana/strawberry with guava juice and protein powder. "Well, something's wrong. Talk to me."

You decide to dive in - what's to lose? This isn't some thug like Gail's trainer—or whatever he is—Pete, or "the Fox", as he likes to be called.

Turn to page 24.

"I don't know. Nothing seems to be right. Nothing seems to work. I'm anxious all the time."

"Why? You're a great athlete. Good student." Bud looks you in the eyes. He seems honest and fair—more than honest and fair.

"I'm worried about the rest of my life; see, I've got to go to college and I don't have the money. My parents are poor."

"No problem. Scholarships are for people like you, great athlete, good student. What are you worried about?"

"I'm just not sure that I am really good enough to really deliver in the big races. I think I'm probably only a flash in the pan, an 'also-ran,' ya know?"

"Well, you are not. Look, maybe I can help. You feel like you don't have that extra edge right? Don't worry, I don't mean illegal drugs, steroids or stuff like that. There are other legal supplements that can give you the edge you need." He looks at you with steady eyes.

You feel a mix of excitement and apprehension. Is he for real? Are there really performance-enhancing substances that really do work and are legal? You have heard that there are and this man doesn't have the crooked look or feel you imagine that pushers probably have.

"Well, how does it work, what do I do?" you ask.

A bunch of kids get up to leave and throw a glance over to you. One waves at the coach. You wonder if they suspect what's going on? But, hey, wait a minute, Bud Devlin said it was legal substances.

Go on to the next page.

Over the next several days you and Bud Devlin get to know each other and you gain more respect and trust in this kind, gentle-but-firm coach. He is definitely becoming your friend—almost an older brother. Your dad has slipped deeper into depression, so he is of no help. You don't want to burden your mom. She has enough on her shoulders.

Bud shows you reports on legal substances, shows you examples of athletes using the substances, but doesn't actually ask you to start using them. No pressure from him. He also helps in your form and style of running. Your times are improving and you feel good—really good.

The big meets are all coming up soon; and one day Bud says to you, "Decision time my friend. Do you want to use the supplements or not?"

If you decide to use them, turn to page 31.

If you decide against using them, turn to page 42.

"Well, you know, I mean I want to win, win big so I can get a college scholarship."

"I do too, my friend," he replies. "We are so poor that only a scholarship will make it possible, and I will still have to work to help support all my brothers and sisters."

"So, I mean, what about doping?"

"A bargain with the devil. Pure and simple. The people who supply the doping substances, are they good people? Are they interested in you? NO! NO! A thousand times. They are interested either in their own career as a trainer or coach or they are making money on the dope or on betting on the races or games. It stinks! It is death disguised as victory."

Antonio is passionate about life, and you are not surprised at the vehemence of his stance against doping. This is actually the way you also feel, and you realize you probably came to ask him just to cement your own position against doping.

"So, how do we win against those who use steroids or amphetamines, or EPO or the other stuff?"

"You must have faith in yourself to begin with. Then hard work and dedication. Those who use drugs will eventually get caught. They always do."

"So, how do we get to college without money?" you ask.

Go on to the next page.

"Athletics are not the only way to scholarships," Antonio says somberly.

"Tell me, I'm all ears."

"You are bright. Very bright. There are academic scholarships. There are loans; there are grants. Open your eyes—look around you!"

He is right, and you know it; but your skills have always been in athletics. That's the easier route, isn't it?

"Also, think about volunteering in the community. I tutor younger kids in math after school once a week for 2 hours."

"Why do that, Antonio?" you ask.

"First, because I want to. I like helping kids. Second, it shows commitment. It's not all about winning games or meets. It's much more."

"You're a math wizard. I'm good at sciences and English. Who do I talk to?" you ask.

"I'll introduce you to my friend who runs the after-school programs."

"But, I don't have the time," you protest.

"Who does? You make time," is his soft reply.

If you decide to do some volunteer teaching, turn to page 28.

If you decide to let it pass for now and stick with athletics, turn to page 5.

You never realized that a day can seem to hold so much more than 24 hours. It's all in how you use your time, how you allocate your energy and interests. So much time is dwindled away, lost, just ignored. A new dimension opens up to you, a dimension of time and space that you never even glimpsed before. You still go to practice, but you shave minutes off both ends, you optimize your workouts, you use what used to be empty minutes to achieve all sorts of things, from homework to isometric exercises, to developing concentration. And you volunteer, teaching first and second graders to read.

Getting the job was as simple as ordering a pizza with mushrooms and anchovies. You expressed interest in volunteer teaching and met the co-ordinator, a really great woman named Naomi Alvarez who runs a town-wide program in reading, writing, and arithmetic for kids at risk—and there are a lot of kids in that group. Kids who don't have strong families, kids who have learning disabilities, kids who at a really young age seem to have already given up, kids who are shy, obnoxious, or just plain bored. She's like an angel to the kids who would otherwise fall between the cracks.

At first the fear of facing a group of kids was intense; but then you saw that they were all scared, all needy, all just kids. You broke it down to one-on-one and concentrated on each kid's needs. One big discovery was that most of what the kids needed was attention. You fell in love with the teaching, and the hours after school in the classroom were magical.

Go on to the next page.

You and Antonio become the closest of friends. His family becomes your family. You feel guilty about not spending so much time at home, but your mom sees that you are happier than you have ever been.

The next 10 months blur past, and although you do well in your races, they are no longer the key to your life. Ms Alvarez gives you both help and guidance. She thinks you are a natural teacher and introduces you to other educators. One day she offers you a paid job to work with kids in several different schools. The trouble is you will have to give up track, there won't be enough time in the day for everything. What to do?

If you take the job, turn to page 69.

If you don't take the job, turn to page 81.

Sometimes it's easier to avoid the really difficult stuff. If you run into Samson in the next couple of days or so, fine. If not, well, time will tell. Maybe it just wasn't to be.

One of the hurdlers, a guy named Jeff, has left the field. You don't like him anyway. He is one self-centered person. Everything he says is about him: how good he is (he really isn't that good), how smart he is (he isn't that smart), and how old and sophisticated he is (he is crude).

That leaves a girl named Isabel and a freshman boy named Fred. She's nice, friendly, but a bit of a Goth. Fred's a nerd and seems to be proud of it. A computer geek and a MMOG super-player, he hurdles well, although awkwardly. You walk over to them trying to look casual or cool, or both.

"Hey, what's happenin'?" you say, the words uncomfortable in your mouth.

The two of them stop talking and, turning around, look at you. Can they read your mind? Is there a rumor that YOU are a druggie? Or are you just being paranoid (a word you have just added to you vocabulary)?

"Uh, not much, actually. Just worried about the big meet coming up," mumbles Fred. He is stretching while he talks, something he always does. You think it's to indicate to others that he is an athlete as well as a geek. Nobody is fooled.

Turn to page 32.

Life can be made up of lots of seemingly little turns and minor decisions, but it can also be made up of big decisions, choices that reach into the future. You have just made a choice that might be the kind that reaches into the future with unforeseen outcomes. You are nervous; it's a bit like being out on the edge of a cliff over a pool of water—150 feet up! Don't look down.

"Coach, how do we start? I mean, what do I do?"

"Simple as eating a pizza," is Devlin's reply. "I've got a supplier who takes all your stats, you know, height, weight, age, and all the tests we have been doing for the last month."

"So, I mean, what's that all about?"

"He has a set of algorithms—you know, equations, formulas, that kind of stuff. He plugs in your data, your events, your latest results, and Bingo! Out comes the correct blend of supplements customized just for you. Neat, isn't it?"

Devlin looks really excited and, as usual, as honest as the day is long (you've never really understood what that old saying means; you'll have to Google it).

"Yeah, sounds cool. When do I get it?"

Turn to page 52.

"Yea, me too," you reply. You find yourself doing a few stretches to try to be in sync with him.

How do you open up this tricky subject? You aren't really close to either of them. You don't belong to any group at school. People see you as a bit of a loner; the truth is you are just too busy, what with sports, studies, and your jobs.

"Didn't I hear that you two are expected to do great this weekend?"

"WE HOPE!" Isabel almost shouts. "Sorry about that. I'm just so nervous. I need something to calm down."

This might be an opening. You go for it.

"I guess you can take stuff to calm down. Ever try it?" you probe.

Both Isabel and Fred give you the weirdest look, as though you had three heads all of different colors or something.

"You've gotta be kidding," Isabel replies. "Valium? Marijuana? That kind of stuff kills the competitive edge."

Fred continues his stretches, which have now almost become contortions.

If you decide to drop the whole thing here, turn to page 70.

If you decide to push on and talk about drug use (doping), turn to page 72.

You wish you had a close friend who you could share your thoughts with. You just haven't had the time for friendship. That's kind of stupid, you know. Time is passing so quickly. Senior year next year, just a few summer months away. Loneliness has been your constant companion, and it feels rotten.

"Okay," you say out loud. "Let's get on with it."

Samson has an office in the athletic building, across the track and baseball fields. You scan for him as you head toward the big, red brick building.

His office is crowded with sports gear, tennis rackets, road bike, lots of books, and pictures on the walls of Samson winning races in school and college. You like the feel of the place, but he is not there. Should you wait for a while? Why not? you decide and take a chair in front of his desk.

The desk is littered with what looks like schedules, maybe for classes, maybe for meets. You hesitate from snooping too much. After all, nobody invited you into his office. You fidget and wish you hadn't decided to come here in the first place.

Turn to page 34.

Then your eyes rest on a neat pile of boxes in the corner partially covered by an old gym bag. Large red letters scream out: GUARANTEED TO IMPROVE —————

Moving quickly to the boxes, you remove the gym bag and read the last word: PERFORMANCE!

A chill runs through you. Samson must be into doping. Here is the evidence. But wait…it would be too obvious, keeping boxes of drugs in his office. *What is this stuff?* you ask yourself. You pick up one of the yellow and red boxes and examine it. Next to the Nutrition Facts, you read:

Peak performance depends on many things. Hydration is one of them. Proper minerals and vitamins. A balance of diet, training, and attitude all lead to peak performance. This product is all natural, contains no stimulants or banned substances, and is a healthy, organic supplement…..

The text continues describing the ingredients and naming athletes and coaches who endorse it. But you don't have time to finish reading it. You can hear Coach Samson's footsteps approaching the office door. What to do?

If you decide to tell him that you want to know more about these supplements, turn to page 35.

If you decide to hide the box and pretend that you were just waiting for him, turn to page 37.

As Coach Samson enters his office, his cell phone chirps out a familiar tune. He opens the phone, motioning for you to take a chair.

"Right. I think I've got another candidate. Yup, sitting in a chair in front of me. Gotta go. Later." He closes the phone and tucks it into his pocket.

"I'm glad you came in. I was going to call you at home and ask to talk to your mom and dad. You see, I've done some research on you, and you are just the kind of kid we want to work with."

You feel uncomfortable. Time to ask questions. And anyway, exactly who is this WE he mentions?

"Why work with me? What kind of work? Why involve my mom and dad?" The questions just tumble out of you.

"Good for you, it's smart to ask questions. I'm a sports medicine doc doing research on increasing performance in young athletes—well, all athletes, actually—naturally with increased health benefits," Samson explains.

"So, why me?"

"You have talent, a good work ethic, you do well academically. Your advisor tells me you are on a college track and that medicine or science of some sort—maybe veterinary school—is your goal." He looks you squarely in the eyes.

Turn to page 36.

"Right. But I'm worried about paying for my college education. It's just not in my family's budget," you reply, now intrigued.

Coach Samson continues. "My wife Linda and I are working together on a study to prove that training, diet, and attitude are superior to steroids, stimulants, and all the other junk around."

"Sure, I'm interested. But—" you hesitate. "What are those boxes? Those supplements over there? They look like drugs to me."

Samson picks one up, opens it, and removes three packets about the size of fruit bars. Each one is a different color. He hands them to you.

"There is nothing special about this. My wife and I believe that supplements and stuff like that aren't useful and can even be dangerous. You don't really know what is in the products. There are very few, if any, controls on most of these supplements."

"So, why do you hand these things out?" you ask, somewhat confused.

"I'm conducting a double-blind controlled experiment with athletes like yourself. It's a harmless powder with a few electrolytes. You see, if you believe you are going to perform well, you probably will. When we reveal that these supplements have nothing in them, then the athlete can see it's about the body, attitude, training."

"Isn't that approach dishonest? I mean you are misleading these kids in your study," you say.

Turn to page 79.

Just in the nick of time you shove the supplement box back under the gym bag and move toward the chair. Coach Samson enters his office and is surprised to find you there.

"Hi! What's up?" He moves to his desk and extends his hand for a firm handshake. His eyes are friendly but there is a look of suspicion on his face. Or maybe you are just feeling guilty. It could be both. But why would the coach have illegal drugs in his office for anyone with half a brain to see?

"I was thinking about what you said the other day. Wanted to talk more about it." You hear the nervousness in your voice. You can't hide it.

"Great. Have a seat."

The phone rings, interrupting the awkwardness of the moment and giving you some time to think what the best next move is.

"Yo! Samson here. What were the results?"

He pauses to listen to a rather long reply to his question. You catch bits and pieces and it sounds like they are referring to blood cells, urine samples, and recovery times.

Are you unwittingly being dragged into doping activity? You've heard stories about how people get hooked into groups and end up both users and pushers.

Turn to page 38.

Standing up, you are about to say that you have to go when the coach holds up his hand to stop you.

"Look, gotta call back. Later." He hangs up the phone and turns to you.

You hesitate, feeling very uncomfortable. This isn't going well. Those boxes seemed to be harmless judging from the info you read on them. Maybe they print false stuff as a cover?

"Coach, I'm late for my job. See you."

"OK."

He leans back in his chair, arms behind his head and looks out the window for a brief moment and speaks just as you reach the doorway.

"You have a lot of promise. I don't mean just in sports. You have talent, brains, and one heck of a future in front of you. Now let's make it all work."

"How? Drugs, doping? I saw those boxes over there. Is that the way I'm suppose to 'make it all work'?"

One moment his face is so serious you think he is about to scream at you and the next he laughs and stands up, arms outstretched.

Turn to page 39.

"You can't be serious! Do you really believe that I'm in favor of doping? You must be kidding."

"But," you stammer. "I mean, it just seems like you talked to me about improving performance and stuff like that."

"So? We can all improve our performance. All of us. I repeat, all of us." He looks deadly serious.

"You didn't know that I'm a sports medicine doctor, did you? This is a part-time job, coaching. It gets me close to the sport I love and close to athletes. I see what improves performance, and both good and bad ways to improve." He motions for you to sit down.

Turn to page 51.

You feel as though you're to jump perched from a high cliff overlooking a rough sea with huge rocks sticking above the water. This is a big decision, and you aren't sure whether you made the right choice.

Gail's mention of some vow disturbs you, it sounds like a gang kind of thing. The Mafia call it omerta, a code of silence and a promise not to get involved with the authorities. You could be getting in over your head. But you asked for this, and now you've got it.

Gail flips open his cell phone and punches a speed-dial number. Whoever he's calling answers right away.

"Can you get here, pronto?" Gail asks. He nods as though the person on the cell is right here in the room. Then he ends the call and looks at you with a big grin on his face.

"Show time, big time, your time! You made the right decision," Gail says, pushing off the couch and going over to the small bookshelf. He picks up a remote, clicks in a command, and gives you a handheld smart phone. It's the latest model—Internet connected, video, phone, search component—you name it, it has it.

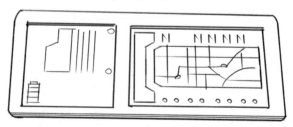

Go on to the next page.

You stare at the thing in your hand; it feels alive as though it will bite you.

"You might as well start learning," Gail announces. His tone is sharp, decisive, and a bit nasty. It's another of his personality changes. "Search performance-enhancing substances," he commands.

Hesitating for just a moment before you obey his command, you feel as though you are already in the air, leaping off the cliff, the rocks and boiling water 150 feet below.

Turn to page 55.

You look away from your friend and coach; you feel as though you are about to betray him. He's invested so much time in you. If you say no and he drops your friendship, you will again face the loneliness that has bothered you for so long. But you just can't accept the supplement use even if it is legal, or at least not illegal. There is something so inherently wrong in taking an advantage over others in a race by using a supplement. You are not a goody-two-shoes; you just believe that some things are right and others absolutely wrong. It's not as though you haven't thought about it—using supplements, even banned ones. You have, but you always come up with total rejection. This way you can live with yourself.

"Hey, Coach?" you start out with. Your voice is scratchy from nervousness at what you are about to do.

"Yeah, I'm here."

"Ah, ah...what cleats or spikes should I use in the race on Saturday?" You have completely ducked the issue. *Coward*, you say to yourself.

Go on to the next page.

"We'll decide on Friday. Weather can play a role. You'll be fine. You're doing great."

"Thanks, Coach."

"Have you thought about my proposal to you? You know, about the supplements?"

Here it is, time for truth. You feel as though the ground underneath you is sinking away and you are free-falling into space. Suddenly your head clears and you feel grounded. Reality is here.

"Yes, coach. Yes, I have. It's not for me. I'm sorry."

Bud Devlin looks at you with a warm smile creasing his sun-burned face.

"Not to worry! It's OK with me. I don't want any pressure on you. You train wonderfully. You are in superb shape. You don't need those supplements anyway. Go for it. Fire it up!"

The relief coming from his generous acceptance of your rejection of his offer to help with supplements is extraordinary; it's like the euphoria of winning a race. But the real test is Saturday, and this race is a big one for you.

Turn to the next page.

44

It's the day of the big race. The butterflies are there as always, but fear has left you. You are confident that win or lose your life goals are on track. You'll get to college one way or another. You are sure of that!

BANG! The starting gun focuses all of your attention—mind, body, soul in the present moment as you race not only against the others but against yourself.

The outcome? You fill this one in.

The End

"Sorry, Coach. I can't do it. I feel fine and that's good enough for this race. Maybe another time."

"Sure, sure. I mean, are you positive? It's good stuff. No harm here."

You shake your head in reply and continue your stretches to prepare for your training session. You know you are right, but it still doesn't feel good to have changed your mind at the last minute. *Oh well, such is life,* you think, as you stretch your hamstrings.

The End

"Here goes nothin'!" you say, as you tip the purple-and-red plastic bottle to your lips and suck down the chocolate-flavored liquid. He was right, it tastes just like a chocolate shake. So...no sudden flashes of lights. No Shazzam! No instant power forces surging in you. Nobody watching, either. Just a good smoothie. You relax. Anyway, there's no sign of "goons from the P-Patrol," as they say.

"Thanks, Coach. Now what?"

"Nothing. It's just good help for your body. You know bodies get depleted from exertion, right? Well, this stuff helps your body replenish more quickly and efficiently, that's all. It facilitates the release of your own natural energy that you can draw on in a race."

"How often do I take it?"

"Daily. We've got 10 days before States; that should be enough time for you to get the maximum benefit from it. You'll do great, I know it."

The rest of the workout goes normally. You think you feel a little more stamina or sharpness, but that could just be the psychological effect of believing that the supplement really works. Anyway, there are no ill side-effects that you can sense. You are running quite well; and Bud Devlin holds up both thumbs at the finish of your last heat. He gives you a huge smile. He has become a really good friend.

Go on to the next page.

Your dream of an athletic scholarship to the local university excites you and seems more and more possible as you rack up impressive wins in many track meets. The States meet is a big one, the biggest for you—and a win here will really look good. You dedicate yourself to preparing for the meet. Rest, good diet, training (but not over-training), technique, and now the legal supplement from Bud Devlin make you feel pretty confident. You are pumped, excited, ready to go!

You dream of success, flashing across the finish line two lengths ahead of the closest runner. You see the medal hanging from your neck, the sports reporters interviewing you, the college admissions officer looking at both your academic record and your track records. You feel better than you ever have in your life. Even your dad seems to perk up, maybe as a result of your energy. He seems more positive about life than he has in years.

"All set?" Devlin asks, handing you the now familiar purple–and–red plastic bottle with the choco-late-flavored drink. He is really proud of you; you are his "secret weapon," his symbol of coaching success, and his poster athlete for legal supplements. You can make his career. Recently, during a conversation when you each expressed your dreams for the future, Devlin had confided to you that he wants to be the head coach of a major university track team and maybe even an Olympic coach. He dangled the Olympic possibility out to you.

"Ya know, kid, you've got the right stuff to make it all the way. Olympics, here we come."

Turn to page 128.

"I didn't know. Sorry, Coach."

"Well, now you do. I can help you improve your performance without doping. Are you with me?"

"Yes, but how?" you ask, brightening.

"First, your body is a marvelous machine or system. What you do with it, how, and what you put in it all count. The boxes you see over there are just powdered electrolytes, nothing more. I use it as a control in my study of performance in young athletes. Believe me, you don't need anything more than balanced nutrition, good training, adequate sleep, and hydration. Then it's up to you alone to perform. Doping is cheating. The list of top athletes caught for doping, stripped of medals, and even going to jail for lying under oath in legal proceedings is long and sad. Think about it."

The End

"I'll have it for you tomorrow. Tastes like a chocolate shake. You'll like it. And is it ever go juice!" Devlin gives you his winning smile. You can't help but like this guy. He's a real friend.

Guilt is like a constant companion for you; it always has been. You don't really know why, because you don't lie, cheat, or steal—okay, maybe a tiny bit. You did take $10 from your mom's purse once. But the feeling that you have done something wrong persists. You wonder if most kids feel this way. Is it the system? Is it human nature? Or are you just a weirdo? At any rate, guilt is one of those persistent, unpleasant, unwanted things. A thought hits you: maybe it's something in your diet. Too much sugar? Too much caffeine from soft drinks or chocolate? Maybe you are allergic to something. Who knows? Life just seems too much sometimes. You are grateful for sports; there's nothing like a good, long, hard workout. It always clears your mind—for awhile, anyhow.

So, on to tomorrow and the chocolate shake!

"Here it is!" Coach Devlin says, holding out a purple-and-red plastic sports bottle. He gives it a good shake before he hands it to you and says, "Enjoy."

You take it and hold it as though it were a poisonous snake. Now's the time. Then again, it's not too late to change your mind, is it?

If at the last moment you decide to refuse it, turn to page 47.

If you open the bottle and drink it down, turn to page 48.

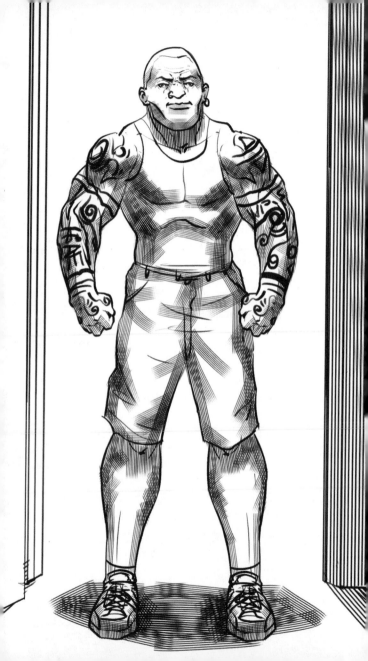

Your fingers fumble on the small keyboard, but you finally key in to find out about performance enhancers. Actually, you have already read up on them. You are worried that you really screwed up by coming here.

The door to the game room opens with not so much as a knock or a hello. A short, squat, heavily muscled man enters. He's got a shaved head, an ear ring, a nose ring, and extensive tattoos on both arms. He looks like a fading bodybuilder, age in the thirties. He smiles sardonically and speaks.

"So this is the new prospect. Way to go, Gail. I knew you would deliver."

You take an instant dislike to this man, almost recoiling as he marches over to you with his meaty hand extended.

"Call me Pete, call me 'Fox'—just don't call me late for dinner," he guffaws.

His handshake is like a vise grip and obviously meant to intimidate. You think he's more like a pig than a fox.

Gail looks a bit nervous and acts as though this creature is his boss.

"Is Foster coming over?" Gail asks.

"We'll see how this goes," the bodybuilder croaks. "We'll see. You ready, kid?" he asks you.

There is an ominous feeling in the room. It's like before a bad storm that's coming in fast.

"For what?" you reply.

Turn to page 56.

Fox looks at Gail. "Hey, I thought you said this was a live one. Doesn't seem so to me."

"It's cool, I mean, you're cool with it, right?" Gail says, nodding at you.

"Yeah, I'm cool with it," you reply, although you don't really know what the 'it' is.

"First things first, I always say," Fox whispers. "Is this place secure?" he asks Gail.

Go on to the next page.

"150%," is Gail's reply.

"Okay, let's get the ceremony over with," Fox says.

Gail clicks a remote and the track curtains slide over windows. He locks the door and turns off the lights after lighting two humongous candles that sit on a glass-and-steel table.

"Come over here," Fox orders.

You obey, carried away by the moment and the sense of ceremony that has taken control of the room. The smell of the candles adds to the mystery; the darkness further combines to make this like some initiation ritual from another age.

Fox stands behind the candles, his hand on a book. *Is it a bible?* you ask yourself. You can't make out what it is. Gail's hand is also on the book.

"Repeat after me," Fox commands. "And put your hand on this book."

You keep thinking how he looks like a pig. The whole thing seems ridiculous.

Turn to page 60.

58

There are lots of books and articles that you find online to help you design a regimen of training and nutrition. You also get guidance from Coach Samson, but you stay far away from Gail. Gail's winning streak is impressive, but you are now competing in different events. You concentrate on the 400; Gail on the sprints. The middle distances can get really technical, but you like the added challenge. It's also somewhat dangerous, if you take a fall in the middle of a pack of runners. But what sport doesn't have some risk?

The 800 demands endurance and technique, using both sprinting and endurance skills. You train harder than you ever have, and it is paying off. Gail is turning on the afterburners in sprints; but there are rumors of a change in his personality, and increased aggression, complete with temper tantrums. Gail is also reported to be driving like a madman. The cops have ticketed Gail twice. Next time it's loss of license. Your friendship has dissolved into barely nodding at each other.

Things at home are no better than they were. Your dad is slipping into depression and taking it out on everybody. His criticisms of you are getting intolerable. You just pray that you will get a scholarship and leave home for college soon.

Turn to page 123.

60

"I promise under the severest of penalties to never reveal my membership in this group, nor other members I might meet, nor what the group represents, nor what it does or provides, nor anything associated with its actions. I do understand that everyone in this group is obligated to help each other when called upon. Failure to do so will result in harsh punishment."

Slowly, Gail repeats Fox's words and asks you to repeat them. You do so, somewhat reluctantly. You feel like a kid spinning around and around to get dizzy—you used to do that until you got sick to your stomach. Before you know it, the brief ceremony is over. There is no merging of blood from pin-pricked fingers, no secret handshakes, no symbols of any kind, just a vow of secrecy under the threat of heavy penalties if broken—maybe even death.

Is this a dream? you wonder. Are you in your right mind?

"The first test for you is to meet Foster. Are you willing?"

"Who is he and why is it a test?" you respond.

"You'll find out. Ya know, you ask too many questions." Fox glares at you through bloodshot eyes.

You could turn back now; it is a risky thing, but if you decide to back out, turn to page 88.

If you decide to meet this Foster guy, turn to page 84.

Access to the school lab allows you, with the help of one of the teachers, to run simple tests on urine and pin-prick blood samples to determine blood-sugar levels, adrenaline level, and other indicators. You develop a comprehensive program that the school approves for course credit. Antonio gives support in statistical correlations. One major pharmaceutical company approaches you to see if you want to be a summer intern.

A strange thing then happens.

Antonio stops helping out in the lab. He seems aloof—not unfriendly exactly, but distant nonetheless.

You confront him one afternoon after about three weeks of this behavior.

"Hey, what's going on?" you ask. He seems taken aback.

"Nothin'," he answers, giving a wan smile. "I'm just busy, really busy. You know, home and the kids, plus my dad isn't doing so well."

"What do you mean? You haven't mentioned your dad. Is he all right?" You haven't been to their house because you have been so busy for several weeks. You are worried. You like his father.

"Well, I didn't want to bother you but my father has had a stroke."

"A stroke!" you exclaim. "How bad? When? Where is he now?" Antonio's father, Alfredo, is a lovely human being and a hard worker. This is really bad news, really bad. He has that big family to support.

Turn to page 92

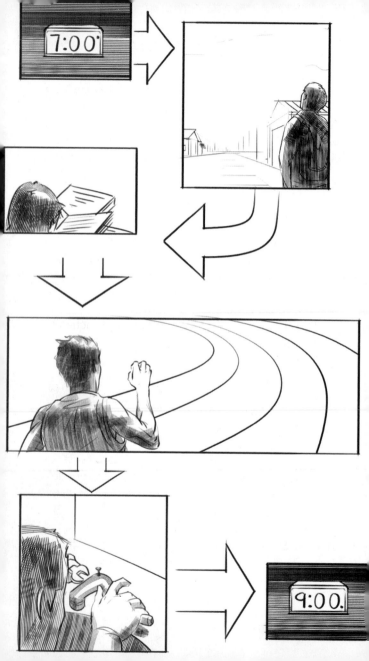

The pressure sure is on! Your junior year in high school is intense. You also have the SATs, day-long exams that can determine your chances of scholarship and entrance to a university. You're sure you will do well on them, but you never know. So every day is study, work to save money, and track. Track is the big one. It focuses your energy; you don't think or worry about anything when you run. It's mind/body stuff and every molecule in your body is focused on reaching the finish line and breaking the tape. You love it, but along with the physical and mental benefits come disappointment and fatigue. Competition can be tough. Results can be uncertain. You sometimes wonder whether or not you are really competitive by nature.

The thought of steroid or other approaches to help your performance hangs over you like some dark cloud. You wish it would go away. You are angry with yourself for even thinking about it, but doping seems to be all around you. Other kids dismiss the bad effects as just stories. A recent book by a former football hero in the US who used steroids shocks some, but other kids say it's just so much propaganda. The footballer used steroids and ended up with heart problems, torn muscles, impotency, enlarged breasts, uncontrollable rage, and psychological issues.

Turn to page 64.

One fact stands out for you, above the rest: steroid use by athletes is often 10 to 100 times the normal amount prescribed by doctors for medical use! *That's outrageous*, you think. Those who sell steroids and other things like amphetamines, human growth hormone, etc., to athletes *must* know that these drugs can have serious adverse side effects. Add to that the fact that these agents are illegal in competition worldwide and can even lead to serious legal problems as well as being kicked off teams for years, and you're left with the question: are they ever worth it?

So, be gone, dark cloud, you wish, but it persists.

Your growth spurt has ended and with it any difficulty you have had with coordination. Now is the time for your greatest performances. Your coaches spur you on, your few friends are admiring of you. You feel good, but—it's a small 'but'—you feel less energetic than you used to. The old get-up-and-go is just not there every day. Your mojo is gone on some days. You try to hide it, but you can't. Finally you make the decision to try steroids.

Before you have an opportunity to put this possibly fateful decision into play, one of your worst fears becomes reality. On a warm, sunny afternoon, just as you're finishing a sprint, you stumble, twist, and SNAP! You sustain a spiral fracture in your leg and your ankle breaks in two. There is little or no pain, but you know what happened. And you know that your career in running is probably over.

The End

Sometimes things—good and bad—seem to come in threes. A week after you decided not to pursue Coach Samson, you are on the track doing sprints. You know you are running very well—body position, arms, and legs working just right. Your breathing is textbook correct. You hydrated carefully, and the carbs you ate the night before—pasta and bread—have kicked in with the metabolized sugar to give you the energy to really pour it on. Even Gail can't catch you today.

Finished with the sprints, you cool down by walking a bit, toweling off your neck, arms, and legs, and slipping on the purple-and-red warm-up jacket with your school's name in big letters across the back. You are really proud of the jacket. It makes you feel a part of everything at the school, and you like the recognition, bragging rights, and pride that come with it. You zip it up tight around your neck, no sense in letting those neck muscles tighten up.

A man who looks like a coach—timing watch on a fob around his neck and clipboard in his hand—approaches.

"Hey, nice running. My name's Pete Loomis."

He holds out his hand to shake. His grip is firm but not overly firm. His smile is generous, but not phony. You can't help but like him from this first impression. But, who is he? You have never seen him before, at least not at school or at practice.

Turn to page 68.

"I'm from the University. Actually, I'm a scout for the track team." He smiles again and seems to wait for your response.

You're caught slightly off-guard. "Oh! That's cool...how can I help you? I'm just a student here. I can introduce you to some of the coaches."

"No, thanks, I already know a lot of them. See, I travel to most of the meets, talk with a lot of kids like you, get to know their coaches. We are looking for real talent. The University wants to build up a reputation for its track team. We're going for the big time."

You know that the University has a very good track team; you have heard that they want to be top-ranked in the world of track. They're looking to recruit Olympic class athletes—and lots of them.

The University has an average reputation for academics, several good graduate departments, and an active alumni association. The School of Environmental Science is gaining a world-class reputation, and the science park close by pumps money in by way of grants, hires professors part-time for specific projects, and supports the University in its applications for government funding. It's growing.

Several years back, the University gave up its football team as too expensive to compete success-fully in its division. So, track rose in importance to bring recognition to the school.

"Well, sounds interesting," you say, trying to play it cool. You are good, everyone says so; but just how good?

Turn to page 102.

After a great deal of thought, you take the job. It pays quite well, and Ms. Alvarez says that it will definitely help you get a scholarship to college. As for track, you drop off the team but keep your foot in the door, so to speak, by training younger kids on Saturday mornings. What a life this is!

You hear rumors that Gail, who is doing very well this year in all the big meets, is doping. You are not surprised, and you are very sorry for him. Then comes the stunning announcement that Gail was killed in a car crash. More rumors of doping and a gang of pushers swirl through school like smoke from a green wood fire. You feel rocked to your roots; it could have been you. You could have got sucked into that grey world of doping and all that it entails. Thanks, Antonio, you think. Thank you for saving my life.

FAST FORWARD 10 YEARS...

You did very well at college in the sciences and went on to veterinary school—all on full scholarships. You kept on teaching kids, something you love and a way to give back to the world.

Now you have your own practice with two other partners and three assistants. Your specialty is small animals, and your reputation has grown by leaps and bounds. You still love to run, but now it's long distance running and even marathons.

Antonio is a college professor, and the two of you see each other often.

The End

"You're right. Actually I get nerved up a lot, too. I try to work out a lot—that way the endorphins kick in and smooth me out." You feel like you're talking too much and too loud—you're a little nervous, feeling that somehow you are in over your head.

Fred stops the contortions, looks at you with his concept of what looking cool is and says, "Well, I'm off. Gotta hit the books. Later."

That leaves you and Isabel. She seems perfectly relaxed, swinging her track shoes by their laces in a slow arc, a smile on her face.

"Okay, what's it all about? Come on." Her tone is kind, not threatening. The two of you have always been friends; you've just never made the time to deepen the friendship.

"I don't know. Scared I guess."

"Of what?" she asks in a low voice.

"Failing," you reply.

"You mean classes? Sports? What?" she presses.

"Everything, I guess. Just havin' a bad day. No big deal."

Isabel nods, stops swinging her shoes, and reaches out to touch your arm.

"You'll be fine. Just fine. Believe me. We all have days like that."

The words of comfort are well intended and feel good, but you know that you have ducked the real issues: doping, sports, cheating. Life.

Go on to the next page.

"You wanna get a juice or something?" she asks.

"That would be great. I'm whipped. Sprints really take it out of me."

"Oh yeah! I've got some apple juice and bananas in my bag over there. Come on."

Isabel comes from a middle-class family. Her mom is an emergency room physician at the nearby hospital and her dad is an accountant at a small firm in the science park. The oldest of three girls, she is popular at school and quite the athlete. She often beats the boys in the high hurdles. Jeff acts like he can't stand her, but a lot of people think he has a big time crush on her.

"What'll it be?" she asks, offering apple juice and some mineral energy drinks.

"Water is fine. Thanks."

The two of you sit quietly on the ground watching pole vaulters and relay-racers practicing hand-offs. Talk just isn't part of the mood. Two friends tired from an already long day.

You missed your chance to talk about what's really on your mind. You ducked the whole issue.

Well, you think, *there is always another day.*

The End

"Look," you say, "I'm...well...I'm concerned about doping." You feel your face get warm and you know that it's getting red. It's always been hard for you to hide your feelings. You worry that they'll take your red face as a sign of guilt or something.

They both look at you, then at each other. There is a communication that passes between them. A hidden message perhaps?

"Concerned? What does that mean? Are you doping?" Fred probes. His face is deadly serious. "Some of us make it on our own, you know."

You wonder why you even brought the subject up. You feel like some kind of a pariah. But there it is. Fred's response tells you that drugs—doping—are scary to a lot of people, and the entire subject brings up strong emotions.

"No, I don't use any of that stuff. But—" you pause.

Isabel looks away for a moment. Fred begins to stretch again in quick jerky movements, almost like karate moves.

"We all are concerned," Fred continues. "I mean, the dopers want to do really well. They want to win at any cost. People like us who don't use are really angry that the users can get a real competitive edge over us. It's not fair. It's dishonest, and worse, it's illegal! And there are other concerns."

Go on to the next page.

You feel Fred and Isabel's anger rising to the surface.

"Like what?" you ask. Now you are getting somewhere.

Isabel looks right into your eyes as though she can enter your soul. She speaks in a calm but powerful voice.

"A lot of kids just don't care or don't know and don't want to know. So, what about you? Why did you come over here? What's really up?"

You decide to put it all out right now.

"I think I'm being approached by someone."

"What for? Someone pushing doping on you?"

You hesitate. Unsure of your ground, feeling cornered and foolish.

"I'm against doping, sure. I mean, it can ruin your health, destroy your career. All that stuff, but I don't really know what's legal and what isn't." You feel stupid.

"You want examples? Is that what you want?" Isabel gives you a knowing look.

*If you decide to bring up Coach Samson,
turn to page 74.*

*If you ask for examples of kids using drugs,
turn to page 76.*

"No. I don't need examples. I mean, I can see what's going on around here. Who can't? Not the stoners. Those drugs don't enhance, they destroy. And it's not only track. Look at the football guys, just about every sport." You feel uncomfortable, but push on. "I want to know what you know or think about Coach Samson."

Silence. No response from either one. Finally Fred speaks.

"Samson? What's he got to do with this? Why him?"

"Well, he said some things to me. I just started to wonder and I saw him with you three and thought maybe you could—"

"Don't lump us in with Jeff. He is one big time jerk! He's a doper. It's more than about winning races for him." Fred rubs his toes into the turf, pawing the grass almost the way a horse would.

Isabel shakes her head. "Easy, Fred. Talk's cheap."

"But back to Samson. Why was the coach talking with you guys? He doesn't coach hurdles, does he?" You watch Isabel's eyes.

"No. No, he doesn't. Is he the one who approached you?"

Go on to the next page.

You are now on the spot. You can either be honest with yourself, or let your suspicions lead you to implicate someone, with potentially serious consequences. Did Coach Samson really approach you about using illegal drugs? No. He never specifically mentioned drugs. He just talked about supplements, food diary, training. Oh, and hydration. He said that hydration was really key in keeping in shape. You just inferred that he was hinting around at illegal performance-enhancing drugs.

"Well, did he or didn't he?" she continues.

"No. No, actually he didn't," you reply.

"Well, so what's up? Are you trying to cause him trouble? Start a rumor? Got a grudge against him or something?"

How do you get out of this mess? You are confused now and they are not making it any easier. You thought Isabel was a friend—someone who would kind of stick up for you, be more understanding.

"I just don't know who to trust these days. I mean, I like Coach Samson from what contact I have with him." Your reply is weak, but honest.

"So, why don't you ask him? Don't ask us. We don't dope. We know a lot of kids do. We don't squeal on anyone. Go ask Samson."

With that, Isabel and Fred walk off. You haven't learned much. You'll have to try something else.

The End

"You really don't know? Seriously? You aren't conning me. You aren't a pusher yourself, are you?" she asks. But her tone is more of concern than anger or dislike.

"Yes, I really do want to know. No, I'm not a pusher. I guess I just feel alone in this. I don't know who else to talk to."

Fred looks embarrassed. Isabel on the other hand seems genuinely concerned.

"Okay. Maybe my mom can fill you in. She's an ER doc, you know. She sees it all: drunks, ODs, physical wrecks, emotional wrecks, busted-up families. It's worse than the TV shows—a lot worse because everything is real: the blood, the ruined lives, and death."

"But I'm talking about doping, not drugs and booze and stuff like that." You know your reply sounds weak, but you weren't prepared for Isabel's speech. She sounds like a teacher and that's not what you want to hear.

"Where do you draw the line?" she continues. "It's all about using and abusing. So, Jeff uses steroids to build up his body, and win races, and don't forget the six pack he loves to show off. He thinks the girls all love it. A lot of them think he's a jerk. And don't forget the 'roidrage' that is a serious side effect of steroids."

"So?"

"So, he's so angry all the time, he's so keyed up he can't tell right from wrong." Isabel starts to cry and then stops as quickly as she started.

"I'm sorry, Isabel," you say, embarrassed at her tears and wondering if you caused them.

Go on to the next page.

"Not your fault. Jeff used to be a great guy. Fun to be around. Mellow. I liked him. We hung out."

"So, what happened?" you ask, knowing the answer.

"Steroids and other junk. He's like a different person. I can't talk with him, can't reach him."

"How long has this been going on?" you ask.

"Oh, about a year. He met some people at a gym he goes to. They were wired into the doping world and convinced him he could be a great star with the help of steroids."

"Don't his coaches know?" you ask, hoping the answer will be a strong repudiation of any involvement by coaches.

"I don't know. I really don't. Anyway, he isn't the only one around here doping."

"Who else?"

"Look, I don't like being a snitch. Open your eyes. Look around. The weight guys—ever see muscles like that on teenagers? How about the sprinters? Notice how some of their times have changed dramatically in the last year?"

"Yeah, but Isabel, we are getting older and stronger. My times have improved and I don't dope."

"Wake up and smell the coffee, dude! The stuff is all over the place. Listen, you don't have to worry about Samson. He's a good guy. I can tell you that." She picks up her backpack and heads off.

"Hey, Isabel, thanks. I didn't mean to upset you. Sorry about that."

"No problem, forget about it. The only thing you don't want to forget is this: Doping is for dopes."

The End

"Let me call my mom, okay?' you reply.

"Sure. Here, you can use my cell."

"Thanks, but I've got my own. Perk of my job at the condos where I work."

"Fine. I've got to talk to the head coach for a moment, so just use my office. Privacy is always a good thing."

Samson gets up and leaves, walking down the hall to the athletic director's office. You are now alone. You hope that you don't get your dad when you call. He doesn't approve of anything you do on your own. He's a control freak, but he's your dad. You like him—or want to—though it's hard.

"In for a penny, in for a pound," you say as you speed dial your house. It's an old expression your mom uses when she makes decisions. You promise yourself to do an Internet search and see where it came from and what it meant in the old days.

You actually keep a file of all the things you look up online. It's fascinating. One separate file is on drugs used to enhance athletic performance. It has been growing lately. You've learned that illegal drugs can be as easy to get as a cup of coffee—non-prescription over-the-counter asthma inhalers, some cold medicines. Even health food supplements can contain illegal substances. Illegal in terms of sports doesn't always mean illicit drugs, such as cocaine or marijuana, but illegal for athletes to use in competition.

Turn to page 120.

"Coach, I'm interested—I mean, who wouldn't be? It's just that I don't have a lot of time to help with your studies. Like right now I'm late for my job."

"I know. How about a different job?" He smiles.

"Like what?" you reply.

"Well, Linda and I work with disabled kids, mostly young kids, with lots of problems both physical and mental. We need an assistant. It could be you."

"Is that why you want to meet my parents?'

"Yes, and also, if you want to be part of a controlled study with these supplements, we would need your parents' permission. We have a grant from a government agency. You and your folks can read the grant forms, talk with the grant administrator in his office, check it all out. What do you think?"

If you need more time to consider,
turn to page 80.

If it all checks out and you decide to sign up,
turn to page 83.

Samson studies your face with an intent look on his face. You avoid looking at him, embarrassed that you are about to give up an offer that seems too good to be true. Mixed emotions flood through you. You think of your parents—how hard your mom works, how depressed your dad is. You really do wish you had a close friend to confide in. Isabel might become a friend, but things didn't end up too well the last time you two spoke.

"Take your time. Don't rush into anything. Think about it. I'd like you to meet Linda. I think you'd like her. As a matter of fact, the two of you are a bit alike: intense, serious, dedicated. Yet, I'll bet you can be really funny at times. Am I right?" He smiles at you.

You want to smile back. You wish his kind words would put you at ease about the whole thing. But you are feeling like the walls are closing in on you. In some ways Samson's proposal seems like the right thing at the right time. But can you really trust him? Part of your problem in making friends has always been the trust thing. Whom can you trust? I mean really trust. It's tough. You even train alone.

Just at that moment, in the late afternoon, with the shadows lengthening on the way to sunset, you hear the sound of jet engines and see a small, silver jet slant across the sky on an approach to the airport. *Is it your morning jet?* you ask yourself. Just for a moment you feel reassured, confident. Optimistic, even. But then you return to Earth.

You hesitate longer, reluctant to answer Samson's probing questions.

Turn to page 82.

Decisions are always tough—well, not always. Sometimes there is a moral imperative that rings like a bell and allows for no evasion. You think about all the absolute NOs that brook no other decision. Murder is one. Betrayal is another. The others, such as cheating, lying, and stealing might have contingencies, you think. "Might" is a weak word, but there could be instances when any one of those words could save a life or serve a worthwhile goal. Maybe. But once down the road to "the end justifies the means," anything can happen, and probably will. That word MIGHT opens up the old barn door and then watch out. *You're getting very philosophical these days,* you say to yourself.

Still, back to your immediate decision: to accept the job working with kids or put that off to some other time.

Reluctantly, you decide to not accept the job right now. There is just too much on your plate, including schoolwork, track, and your job at the condos. Priorities, it's all about priorities. Right now the big one is to get a scholarship to college. Your studies and track performance should be your top priority.

Turn to page 63.

"Coach, I think I'd better take some time to think it over. I'm a little confused about where my life is going. I appreciate your offer, I really do."

He nods and leans a bit toward you.

"Not to worry. I'm always here. I will always listen. The offer is good for a week or so, but I really do need an assistant. I think you'd be great. But if it doesn't feel right, don't do it. Okay?" He holds out his hand and gives a firm shake. There are smile lines around his eyes and mouth.

"Right. Thanks," you murmur.

On your walk home you go over everything he said, examining it and your excitement and hesitations.

"I think I'm a damned fool!" you say out loud.

An elderly couple coming out of Len's Bar-B-Q look up as though you were talking to them. They shake their heads as if to say, "What's with this modern generation?"

You pick up your pace. You'll give it more thought. You're sure of that.

The End

"I'd like to work for you," you answer. You are running on instinct now, but you can check up on Samson and his wife and back out of this deal at any time. Your mom will help; she's really astute about such things. She'll know how to vet Samson and be sure he's legitimate. Life gets complicated, you think, but great opportunities don't happen all the time. What was that expression, a Latin phrase. *Caveat emptor.* Doesn't it mean "seize the day"?

Samson smiles, picks up his cell phone, and punches in a pre-set number. You hear it ring. It's picked up on the third ring. You are nervous and excited at the same time.

"Hi, Honey! Just talked to our young friend. Yup, the one I've mentioned several times. Great candidate for us. What's that? All three of us? Hold on."

Several kids you recognize stop by the office and wave at Samson. "We'll be back later, coach," a red haired girl in vile green sweat clothes says. Samson waves back, smiling his great smile.

Now he turns to you.

"Linda would like the three of us to meet. You'll like her, I'm sure."

"When?" you reply. Things are moving fast, faster than you like. But maybe you've always been too cautious. On the other hand, caution is a good thing.

"Well, how about later today?"

Turn to page 78.

"Sure, I'll meet Foster. How do I get there?" you ask.

"We'll call a cab. It'll be here in a few. Help yourself to some food or stuff."

Fox moves to the side of the room, now ignoring you. Gail seems to have lost most of his usual vigor. He offers a can of organic fruit juice and a plate of sandwiches that the cook left for you. It tastes good, and you enjoy the relief that comes when a difficult decision is made.

"Ever met Foster?" you ask Gail. Anxiety isn't totally gone.

"We don't talk about him or others. Got it? Remember the vow? We aren't kidding."

"10-4." You don't like this one bit. You have a feeling that something weird is going down. But, maybe this is the price you have to pay to really join the "big time."

Fox turns back to you and Gail.

"Cab's here. Take this," he says, shoving a $50 bill into your hand. "Remember, Mr. Foster expects you right away. Got it?" Fox is so gruff. You figure he dislikes you as much as you dislike him; but you don't have to like the people you work with, right? Not if they can help you get where you want to go.

Turn to page 86.

You decide to risk your friendship with Antonio by showing him that you are concerned for his well-being and confronting him about your strong suspicions that he is doping. So, here goes!

Antonio finishes his workout late while you are just arriving at the track field. He is talking with two people who occasionally show up for meets and talk to some of the coaches and some of the runners. You don't know who they are, but they seem innocent enough. You worry that you are getting paranoid about everything. Stories about your old friend Gail's involvement with a doping gang sound real and scary. There are bad people in the world, that's for sure.

"Hey, Toni!" you cry, waving your hands as you walk quickly toward him. "It's me!"

Antonio acknowledges you and leaves the man and the woman he was talking with.

There is a smile on his face, a big one. You haven't seen this in a while. You feel a wave of relief settle on you.

"How's your dad?"

"Better, a little. You know, it takes time."

"Your brothers and sisters and mom?"

"All good. See, I got this job working for those two people over there." He points to the man and woman he was talking with. "It's simple, doesn't take much time and pays really good, really good."

"What is it?" you ask.

"Oh, you know, I'm quick with numbers, so I do Excel spread sheets, computer stuff like business plans, analysis of reports and numbers. Stuff like that. Fun, easy, nothing sexy."

Turn to page 99.

Twenty-five minutes later you stand in front of a handsome, grey-haired man in an immaculately cut suit. His office is very large, more like a living room than an office. There are no papers on his desk. You wonder what he does. There is a secretary going over some papers, but no one else around. The walls are covered with sporting pictures, including horse racing, cycling, tennis, golf, baseball. No track shots, though.

Mr. Foster smiles broadly. "Sit down. Glad you're here. Would you care for a beverage? We've got fruit juices, plain water, herb tea." He points to a glass bowl filled with apples and pears. "Help yourself to some fruit."

He turns to his secretary. "Mary, could you leave us alone for awhile?"

She smiles, nods to you, and leaves. You hear the click of the door and suddenly feel frightened. This man is too smooth, too confident, too obliging. What's his game? This might be much more than you ever bargained for. It's straight out of a TV drama, and a low-budget one at that.

Mr. Foster fiddles with a tennis ball, rolling it between his large fingers. He seems lost in thought. Finally, after several long minutes, he stops fiddling with the tennis ball and turns directly to you. The smile is gone. He begins to speak, and you are shocked by what he says.

Go on to the next page.

"We want you to be an undercover agent."

"A—a what?" you stammer. Who is this guy?

"Mr. Foster is my alias, my real name is irrelevant. Suffice it to say that I am a federal agent. I'm in charge of a sting operation to uncover and prosecute dealers of sports drugs or performance-enhancing agents. This is big business and causes a lot of harm to young people worldwide—not just physical harm, but also personal and social harm—I mean, harm to society. It ruins careers. It destroys opportunities. It's rotten to the core. But we can't prosecute without proof of illegal acts. Dealing. Recruiting people like you to use these substances—some of which are not illegal."

The speech is long, but seems to be a laser beam of straight talk. *Are you being framed?* you ask yourself. You haven't even used any of these substances, and never ever in a competition. You were just trying to find out about it.

"I—I—I never did anything," you whisper; fear has you in its grip.

"Didn't say you did, did I?" Foster or whatever-his-name-is replies. "Look, we know all about you. Here's a file on you. You're as clean as a whistle. Good kid all around. When you approached Gail, we tracked you. Gail's house is wired, or at least his game room is. His cell is wired as well. The guy who calls himself 'Fox,' his cell's wired as well. You are in bad, bad company."

"So, what can I do? I never thought I'd get tangled up in anything like this. I mean, this is scary."

Turn to page 119

You make the judgment that the whole vow business is fake—just a way of scaring you. You hope you are right. The threat of severe punishment—even death!—seems like the script for a bad TV show, but if you are wrong, you are in deep trouble.

Could just using steroids or other performance-enhancing stuff be that serious? That dangerous? There is so much talk about winning, getting the most out of your body, looking great, etc. Kids brag about using just like they brag about taking risks, as if risk-taking were real macho, and being a straight arrow is for wusses. Well, you bet none of these kids have been in the position you are now: initiated into some unknown secret club that threatens you. All you wanted to do was find out a little bit more about your options. You never expected to get mixed up in something like this.

How do you get out? The door is locked. Gail seems nervous and acts like he doesn't even know you. The creature called Fox looks like an enforcer, a hit-man. For all you know, he could be carrying a weapon. This is getting to be more like a nightmare by the minute.

Go on to the next page.

"So, what's next, I mean, what do I do right now?"

"Nervy, aren't you?" Fox says.

Gail seems to get in control of himself again. He moves over to the light switches and once again the game room is filled with light and looks innocuous except for the still-burning candles on the table. Fox snuffs them out.

"Here's the deal: You take this package and deliver it to Foster. The address is 931 Redstone Terrace, 32nd floor, Suite 6A. Got it? Don't write it down. Hurry. He's waiting."

"What's in the package?" you ask, surprised that you would risk asking.

Fox's bloodshot eyes almost bulge right out of his porcine head.

"Zip it, you airhead! Are you nuts? No questions!" He turns to Gail. "Maybe we made a mistake—rather, maybe you made a mistake. Airhead here seems to be nothing but trouble."

"It'll be fine. It's cool, right?" he says to you.

You nod. It's all you can muster. This is getting dangerous fast.

"Okay, let's get this over with," Gail mutters.

"Go with him, Gail. No screw-ups. Got it?"

"Sure, sure." Gail doesn't look like a Golden Boy anymore; he looks like a scared kid.

Turn to page 90.

The package is a small, common looking FedEx mailer, sealed tightly. What's in it, you can only imagine.

Moments later you breathe a sigh of relief as you and Gail leave his monster house, climb into his apple-red car, and head for downtown and the mysterious Foster.

"Hey, Gail, are you feeling what I'm feeling?" you venture.

Gail doesn't respond. He stares straight ahead at the road, ignoring you. You can't read his mood. Anger, resentment, fear? *What's going on?* you ask yourself.

Ten minutes later, nearing the exit for the city, you and Gail both notice a dark grey sedan with dark tinted windows riding alongside you, very close—way too close for comfort.

"Who's that, Gail?" you ask.

Gail doesn't answer but accelerates and cuts the angle to the exit re-joining the highway traffic, narrowly missing a collision with a truck. The trucks blares its horn and swerves into another lane.

"Are you crazy? This is nuts! What's going on?!"

"You don't get it, do you?" he replies grimly, hanging on to the wheel and careening down the highway. The grey sedan is beginning to catch up.

Go on to the next page.

Moments later you hear a splintering smack and the windshield shatters into a thousand cracks with a hole the size of a fist right by your head.

"This is for real!" you scream just as another bullet smacks into the car. A volley of shots follows. It's got to be a machine pistol, probably a 9mm Glock or something like it you think.

Gail slumps over the wheel. He's been shot dead! The car spins out of control, smashes into the guardrails, flips, and screeches to a grinding halt 50 or more yards down the highway. Vehicles swerve frantically to avoid hitting your car.

Months later, in rehab for multiple leg fractures and head injury, you try to piece together what really happened. The police interviewed you repeatedly. Steroids and growth hormones, speed, and other illegal substances were found in Gail's car. The package to Foster apparently contained nothing but cut-up newspaper.

What were Gail and that creep Fox really into? Whatever it was, the price was so high that death was one of the payoffs. You've also paid a very high price—your reputation has been irrevocably damaged because you were in the car with Gail, and your legs will never carry you to victory again. You're finished.

The End

"Home...uh...he's not too bad. He'll be fine." There is evasion in Antonio's voice. Something is up. You are sure of it now.

"I'm coming over tonight," you announce. There is no room for discussion, and Antonio puts up no resistance.

Alfredo sits by the small woodstove in his favorite living room chair, watching TV. He greets you with the wave of his left arm. His right arm rests immobile on his lap. His face seems frozen into a half smile.

"Goo—oo—d to seeeeeee you, f-f-friend of m-y son," he manages.

This is worse than you thought. Alfredo needs rehab badly. Also, what about money to keep the family going? Is there insurance? Are there jobless benefits? Can his wife, Josefina, leave the kids in order to work? These questions flood your brain. No wonder Antonio has been scarce. But why didn't he tell you? You are tight—really close friends. Or so you thought.

Antonio takes you aside.

"Things are fine. There is money for all our needs. It has been taken care of. Not to worry."

Again, the feeling that this is not the whole story fills you. It is an uneasy feeling. Surely this is a bad situation that is not going to get better anytime soon.

"Sure, sure. Glad that everything's okay. Well, gotta get going. Tell your folks I said goodbye." You leave, saddened by what you saw.

Turn to page 94.

Just at that very moment an RV drives up and parks right in front of the athletic building. Three people, holding clipboards and looking very official, get out, open the back door, draw out steps, and put up a sign that reads: Doping Control Station. Loomis jumps to his feet.

"I'm out of here. You don't want to mess with those guys."

Loomis leaves you and Gail sitting at the table. It is as if he had never been there, except for his empty teacup.

"What's this all about?" you ask Gail.

"About winning. It's all about winning, after all, isn't it?' Gail finishes his soda.

"I don't know. I mean, winning, always winning. By any means. Isn't that what old Howard Boardman used to say in history class—that more trouble in the world has been caused by the expression 'The End Justifies the Means'?" You liked your history teacher; but he preached a lot in class. Too much, many thought.

"Don't sweat it. Geez, you're so uptight you wouldn't recognize a rainbow when you saw it." Gail looks away, shaking his head in disapproval, and gets ready to go.

Turn to page 106.

94

Antonio stays apart from you more and more. He seems withdrawn, somber, evasive. But his performance on the track is excellent. Antonio blows everybody away in the 60 and the 100-meter dash. He is magical. He is a hero to everybody. Still, he does not seem relaxed or confident. *What is it?* you ask yourself. *Is he doping? Is it steroids or other junk? Does that account for his performance?*

Summer comes on with the suddenness of a thunderstorm. Boom—you get through final exams, school's out, and it's technically "vacation," but you want to make money, so you put in even more hours at your maintenance job at the condos. You are diligent about track. You take on assignments from a pharmaceutical company to do reports on athletic performances from data they supply to you. It seems legitimate, and your teacher agrees that it is okay.

Antonio is getting great press for his speed; and the big event of the summer is an open track meet about 200 miles away. You still don't see much of him, but he seems to be fine. You asked him a couple of times if he wanted any blood or urine work-ups but he declined. You hope with all your might he isn't using drugs.

Turn to page 98.

Foster (or whatever his name is) stares out the window looking at the high-rise office park, the condominiums, the lake, and the rolling hills beyond. He seems lost in a daydream; then he snaps back to reality.

"Money, greed. It's all about that, isn't it? Look, anabolic steroids, human growth hormones, blood doping, amphetamines, you name it—anything that can give someone an edge in competition is invaluable. Many of these substances are banned by WADA and, in many countries, are controlled substances. You know what that means?"

"What?" you ask. You think you know but you're not sure.

"Simple, controlled substances are prescription-based or outright illegal like cocaine, pot, etc. But steroids and HGH and other things are also controlled in many countries. You are fooling with the law as well as the rules of WADA, the IOC, and other sports organizations. It's a one-way street to trouble. Sounds like a lecture doesn't it?"

"Yeah, it does." Adults are always lecturing kids; that's why the kids often don't listen, you think. Blah, blah, blah!"

"Well, people get killed in this racket—I don't mean dying from substance abuse, though that does occur—I mean, where there is a lot of fast money, there are bad people. Don't get in their way."

"Oh, come on. This sounds like a TV drama." But you are wary of the whole thing. "Foster" does make some good points, even though he is an adult.

Go on to the next page.

"I told you this could be dangerous. You still want in?"

"Yes, I'm in." You know that you have to help. There are times in a person's life when a choice, a decision, a commitment must be made. This is a big one.

Foster paces the room, obviously worried. "We need your parents to sign off on this. Will they?"

"I don't know. I'll try." This could be your way out of the whole mess!

If you decide to tell your mom and ask her not to agree to your participation in the sting, turn to page 115.

If you decide to tell your mom that it's a research project or something so that she'll give permission, turn to page 129.

As his friend you consider it your personal responsibility to confront Antonio and tell him that you are worried that he is doping. But his lack of communication with you makes you wary of a direct confrontation. The part of you that is the loner just wants to avoid confrontation. After all, it's his problem, you think. He knows where you are and can seek your help or advice any time.

*If you decide to confront him,
turn to page 85.*

If you let it pass, turn to page 101.

You feel relieved again, pleased that he is using his skills and getting paid well. Knowing Antonio, you are sure he's using the money to help his family. He truly is a generous person.

The question remains: should you confront him about doping? In your worldview, the answer is an unequivocal yes.

"Antonio, look, I mean, we're friends, right?"

He nods enthusiastically; you sense he knows what's coming.

"Antonio, I'm worried that you might be doping." Your words fall like stones on a marble floor. Antonio stares at you.

"How? Why would you think that? No, a thousand times NO!"

"But, I mean, you don't want my help; most of the time you avoid me; you look depressed."

"I just have a lot on my mind. Not to worry. I do not—repeat—do not use dope."

"Great! Good luck in the big meet. It's this weekend, isn't it?"

"Yes. I'm ready. I have had the best times ever. My friends—the ones I do the work for—they have been tracking my performance. They love track. Are you running?"

"No," you reply. "Too busy right now. Good luck to you."

Turn to the next page.

Then things turn bad, really bad for Antonio. Instead of winning at the big race, he comes in a dismal fifth, way out of the running. His performance is so far off that he is subjected to testing. Unfortunately his blood and urine samples show evidence of muscle relaxants and tranquilizers—a sure prescription for failure.

Within days, the FBI announces that they have uncovered a betting syndicate that uses either payoffs or drugs to manipulate results in all sorts of sporting events. It's happened in tennis, basketball, soccer, you name it.

At first, Antonio was mentioned as a target for the investigation. After months of investigation he was cleared of any wrongdoing. The slow-down cocktail was given to him in a banana smoothie by one of two so-called "friends" he worked for. They were part of the syndicate and face jail sentences.

Antonio finished high school and college, and went on to The Institute For Advanced Studies at Princeton University on a full scholarship. He is now a professor of advanced mathematics at the University of California, Berkeley. The two of you remain friends to this day.

The End

You are uncomfortable with your decision not to confront Antonio about doping. So, you reverse field and plan to talk with him.

Turn to page 85.

"We are careful who we pick. It can be a very attractive package for you."

The two of you are walking toward the athletic center. You nod at several other students as they pass by; they give you a curious, seemingly knowing look. Could it be the man you are walking with? Do they know something about him?

Your friend Gail comes running up to the two of you. Grinning and slapping you on the shoulder, Gail says, "Hey, any chance I can join you two?"

Gail has always been bold and upfront, but lately his behavior has been overly aggressive, or so it seems to you. You attribute it to just being a guy, acting tough, doing the alpha-male thing. You're not sure how to reply, but Loomis prevents an awkward moment by speaking up.

"Sure. Come on over and have a fruit juice or a water or whatever you want. It's on me."

"How're you doin'? I'm Gail." They shake hands.

"I know who you are. Glad to meet you. I was going to look you up in a day or two. Looks like your timing is impeccable."

You feel upstaged by Gail; it's always been that way. He's rich, liked by everyone, drives a cool car, and loves to dominate. You know that you are a better scholar and athlete than he is, but you still feel in Gail's shadow. It's tough being a teenager.

Go on to the next page.

There is a small snack bar in the athletic building and today it is jammed with kids and coaches. The snack bar serves up great banana smoothies, but also sugar-laden soda and potato chips. Gail goes for a soda and a bag of chips; you watch Loomis's eyes to see his reaction, but he's a careful man, hard to read. You go for the banana smoothie. The potassium in the banana helps with the cramps that often plague you.

The talk begins easy and comfortably, focusing on great track stars, records made and broken, new techniques, even equipment issues for pole vaulters. No big deal, you think.

Then, suddenly, the tenor of the talk shifts. Loomis mentions the names of several Olympic athletes caught for drug use—big names like Marion Jones in track, Floyd Landis in the Tour de France, and several others in those tough, grueling, demanding sports that have been riddled with drug or doping abuse. You don't know where he is going with this.

"So, you two, what do you think?" he asks, looking as earnest as possible.

"What do you mean?" you ask.

Gail jumps in.

"They were stupid. Used the wrong stuff. Got caught," he says.

Both of them look at you, waiting for your reply. It's as if the two of them were on the same side watching to see if you were going to join them.

If you decide to play along and see where it goes, turn to page 93.

If you decide to say what you really feel, turn to page 105.

There is a brief moment when both of them survey you, waiting for your response. You let the moment dangle, enjoying the building tension.

"I don't quite get you. I mean, are you suggesting that there are performance-enhancers—drugs, supplements, other stuff—that can't be detected?"

You scan their faces. Both look blank, then glance at each other. Gail speaks first.

"Hey, no big deal. Any edge is worth doing sometimes." He leans back in his chair and sips his soda.

Loomis picks up where Gail left off.

"There are lots of things we know and lots of things we don't know about enhancing performance. Let's put it this way: if you want to be the best, it's not enough just to want it, you have to make training your highest priority, which means giving up stuff like an active social life. You have to push yourself like you've never done before, and take risks. Right?"

"Okay," you nod. You don't like where this is going.

Loomis makes a steeple out of his fingers, studies it, and then says, "Look, if it's not illegal, then we say it's a go. Use it. If it becomes illegal, then stop. Are you with me?"

"Nope, I'm not. I'm nobody's guinea pig. Not for a university, not for a drug company, not for a team. That's it."

Loomis gets up, extends his hand. You shake and he says, "Good luck. You're going to need it."

Gail hesitates, gives you a snarky look, and in a low voice, hisses, "you are a such a wuss! I had hopes for you, but—."

The End

"Wait a sec, Gail. Tell me, just where does this all lead to? I mean, we're doing well right now, aren't we?'

"Ask yourself. Are you gonna win all your races? Are you gonna be the star?" Gail hesitates and then picks up his purple-and-red athletic bag and heads for the door.

"So, are you using steroids?" you blurt out. "Because if you are, you run a risk of getting caught."

The WADA (World Anti-Doping Agency) promotes drug-free sports. It's the concept of the level playing field—everyone gets a fair chance, no cutting corners with substances that increase performance. Far from being policemen, WADA helps insure that the playing fields are level. International sport federations and anti-doping organizations are responsible for collecting urine and/or blood samples from athletes.

"Buzz off! Mind your own business, you twerp." Gail's voice is strained and angry now. His face is turning red, eyes glaring. He sneers at you through gritted teeth. "What do you know? Nothin'!"

"I know that athletic associations select and test athletes at random for doping—or drugs as you call it—or automatically test the top athletes in any event."

Go on to the next page.

You try to keep Gail engaged, hoping he'll be pulled in for testing. "Remember the pledge we all signed at school to refrain from using illegal substances of any kind? The pledge made it clear that illegal substances found in urine or blood samples would immediately result in two years' expulsion from the team. The pledge also listed the types of drugs in categories. There was also a description of the possible side effects of the use of drugs like anabolic steroids, erythropoietin, or 'EPO', stimulants, all that stuff."

"Blah, blah, blah! Get a life! I'm outta here!" Gail storms off.

Turn to page 108.

108

You sit at the table watching some kids being pulled in for testing. You never know when it's going to happen, except for maybe the big meets. Today it's the turn for about 6 kids. You're not one of them. You notice that no one seems to refuse, but you noticed two kids from the lacrosse team looking worried the minute they were approached by the doping control people. You assume that they must have known what it was about.

One of the kids was the team captain. He is a star, scoring goals in every game. His muscles are the envy of everyone in school—both the boys and the girls. Could they be the result of steroids? Some people think they must be.

The rest of the season is fairly good for you. You win more than your fair share of the races, at least placing in the top three. You see Loomis now and then, but neither one of you make any attempt at contact. Gail continues to hang around him. *Why would the University hire a creep like that?* you ask yourself. The regular coaches don't seem to have much to do with him. You don't like him; you have always followed your gut instincts, and they have rarely let you down.

Turn to page 58.

Surprisingly, escaping from this madhouse is as easy as eating a slice of pizza. You just turn around and walk out the way you came. The screams stop abruptly. Maybe they had come from a TV in another room. Maybe not.

You expect to hear Fox running after you, or even a gunshot or a yell.

Nothing. You just exit into the fading sunlight of late afternoon. You wonder if Foster's people really did have you 'covered.' It's all like some dream.

You make tracks for home, but you are tormented by the fear that Fox and his gang will never leave you alone. You know too much. You wonder about Foster. Will he just let you walk away?

Two days later an announcement comes over the school PA system asking all students to go to your homerooms. You wonder whether there is a national crisis or something.

The principal comes on the PA in a somber voice to announce that Gail Forbes has died in an automobile accident early this morning. The chief of police comes on to announce that Gail had been the object of a dangerous high speed chase by police, who saw him driving erratically on the interstate. You wonder why they gave the details, but maybe it was seen as a warning to other kids.

"Dudes, they're talking about roidrage. Gail was going nuts lately," a kid in your class announces to the others.

There are murmurs of agreement, sadness, shock, anger, tears, and disbelief. Gail had been a Golden Boy, and now he is gone.

Turn to page 112.

The minute the PA ends, the room erupts into a buzz loud enough to drown out a heavy metal band at full volume.

"Gail's dead! Can you believe it?!"

"No way, the guy's a god!"

"This can't be happening!"

"Life's short."

"He was always pushing it."

Some people are stunned speechless, some are crying; one girl sobs uncontrollably. *Was she Gail's girlfriend?* you wonder. In the past few weeks, various rumors had been swirling around Gail— that he had dumped his girlfriend, that he was no longer interested in girls, that maybe he was gay. You figured the rumors started because people were confused about Gail's personality changes— aggression, anger, fits of rage.

More sensible rumors—but rumors nonetheless—blamed his personality changes on drug usage: EPO, HGH, anabolic steroids. More rumors said steroid use could lead to impotency and loss of sex drive.

Gaggles of kids come in from other rooms seeking the comfort of friends.

Five days later there is a funeral for Gail. His parents look devastated. Who knows—maybe they really did love him, maybe they really did care.

The End

114

You are not really sure that waiting for these dudes is the smartest, but you do. It doesn't take long before Fox—or "Piggy", in your mind—bounces back in. A sneer is scribed across his porcine face.

"So, weisenheimer, you passed the big test. Foster gives you a thumbs up."

He waits for your reaction; but you play it cool.

"Hey! You deaf?! Didn't you hear what I said? Listen up. You're in. Now you gotta work the kids on the team. We'll cut you in on every kid you sign up for 'roids. Could be decent bucks."

"Whatever," you reply. It isn't a remark you usually use—too rude for your style.

At that moment Gail reappears, and he doesn't look any too happy. He looks as though he has been through a meat grinder. Fox must have pressured him or threatened him or who knows what.

You give a nod and a wave to Gail, but he ignores you and heads for the door.

"Just where do you think you're going?" Fox shouts menacingly.

"Out! Away from this insanity!" Gail races from the room, down the hall and out to his car.

Amazingly, Fox doesn't seem to take this behavior too seriously. He smirks at you and sits down.

"He'll be back. Mark my words. A little rebellion is a good thing, I always say. And remember this: our group doesn't forget and we don't forgive, either. Got it?"

Turn to page 116.

"Sounds good," Foster replies. "I'll have Stella run you home. Time is of the essence. Go for it."

There is something about Foster that just doesn't sound right. He is too glib, too facile. This is your way out. But what about Fox and his group? Maybe you can get Foster to say that he doesn't approve of you. That could get you off the hook. Still, it's a dangerous mess.

Your mom listens, grows very concerned and says, "Honey, maybe we should check this whole thing out. It sounds a bit fishy. After all, this Foster or whoever he is, is he really doing a sting operation with the Feds? You can dummy up documents real easy these days."

"Mom, I just want out. I think all you have to do is write a letter refusing permission for me to join this operation and it's over."

"Things are never as easy as they seem. But let's give it a shot."

She writes the letter and you deliver it. You hope it's the end of the whole mess, but you have a feeling it isn't.

The End

You don't like any of this. Sports are supposed to be clean, a representation of the best in people. Sports are not about cheating, about grabbing tons of money—or are they? The top players get tons of money—multimillion dollar contracts, not to mention what they pull in for endorsing commercial products. Corruption is at all levels, but—and this is the big but—good people are in the mix, too. Really good people, who play by the rules.

Look at all of the clean athletes out there. There are lots of them—all stars, all drug-free, not in anybody's pocket—just pure athleticism. Isn't that what it's all about: pure competition? You look at Fox, thinking here I am, watching this animal who makes money off young people by selling drugs and other performance-enhancing substances, by betting on races that are fixed. This is not for you. You hope it's not for Gail, either, but you are worried.

Your thoughts are disrupted by the sound of Gail's car roaring away with a screech of tires. Fox jerks his thumb at the door and says in a half-grunt, "Nut job. One day he'll kill himself in that speed bucket."

And that is just what happens. But not before Fox and his gang are nailed by the Feds. Good job!

The End

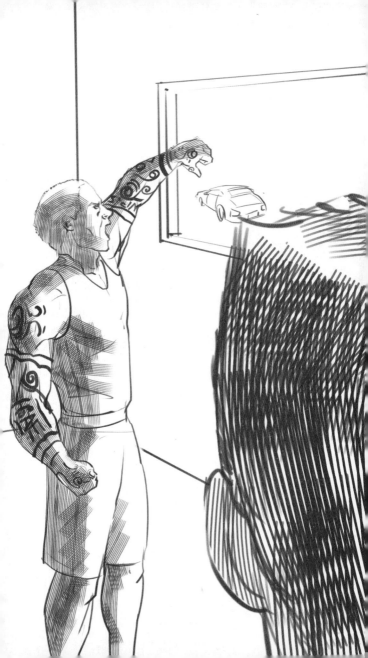

"Yes, it is scary. We want you to carry on with them, just act normal. We need hard evidence. You have already provided some, even though you didn't know it."

"How?"

"The package you brought. It's phony—just a bunch of cut-up newspaper; but what you didn't know was that they slipped two ounces of pure cocaine into your jacket pocket. Go ahead. Check it." "Foster" is deadly serious.

Sure enough, there is a small plastic bag enclosing a smaller plastic bag with white powder in it. It's in your side pocket.

Flash!

Foster holds a digital camera; he has just taken a photo of you holding the bag with the cocaine. What is going on?!

"Not to worry. This is part of the plan. I take a picture of you holding the smack. Fox and his gang believe that we now have you tied to us—by 'us' I mean this gang—with evidence that you are a dealer or the very least a courier. Don't worry. If you join the sting operation I'm running, you are totally protected. Okay?"

This is the second time in hours that you have been asked to join a group or a gang or an organization, basically against your will.

"Here are my credentials," "Foster" says, holding out a wallet with a federal ID. Is it genuine? Who knows?

Turn to page 96.

120

Ignorance of what is in a supplement doesn't get anybody off the hook if it shows up in a urine or blood test. You had better know exactly what you are putting into your body. A simple flu remedy might be enough to show up as doping. Careers can be ruined overnight. This is not child's play. This is for real.

Your mom picks up on the first ring. She's home from work early; you hope that there is nothing wrong.

"Hi, honey, what's up?" she asks.

"Mom, I've got this great opportunity. At least I think it's great. But, I need your advice."

"Go ahead—I have time to listen."

She listens patiently while you go through the whole story.

"So, Mom, what should I do? Will you help?"

She pauses, then says, "Wow, this is a tricky one, isn't it? Sometimes it's best to do things on your own, which I know you tend to like to do. Other times you can gain a lot with the help of a mentor. Follow your heart, follow your gut, trust your instincts, own the decision. I have faith in you."

You know she is right. Adulthood is knocking. Anyway, you can always back out.

If you decide to wait for the next big opportunity, turn to page 121.

If you decide to jump in with both feet, turn to page 122.

Years later, when you are a successful veterinarian running your own office with six other assistants in a large city not far from where you grew up, you think about your life and your decisions.

You passed on the opportunity with Coach Samson and did it on your own. He remained interested in you and offered advice and friendship during your senior year in high school. Another student worked with him and his wife and did very well. Samson was honest and trustworthy, but you liked making it on your own.

Working with animals, you have studied the affects of drugs and still wonder why young athletes will take huge risks with their bodies. There are better ways to perform well.

The End

122

The world opened up to you by Coach Samson turns out to be amazing beyond belief. They have been well funded to do research on doping and its effects both short—and long-term.

Participating in the studies is a huge commitment of time and energy, and you travel all over the state interviewing coaches and athletes. Samson and his wife are convinced that diet, nutrition, training, and attitude are the keys to peak performance on the field and in the classroom. Your research team measures and evaluates the relationship between individual athletic performance and diet, training regimen, and psychological profile.

Your mom becomes a friend of Samson and Linda as well, but your dad still takes a dim view of depending on others. His business opportunities seem to vanish like frost on a window pane after the sun hits it. You are sorry for him, and you do succeed in talking more to him, almost adult to adult.

Your desire to compete diminishes considerably, mainly because you have turned your focus to the research for the study Samson and Linda have underway. You have become an important part of that team.

Never really close to Gail and Antonio, you watch from a distance as they pursue their goals on the field and in school.

Turn to page 125.

Surprising events happen later in the season. The tri-state meet is upon you. The best athletes are all there to compete for fame and bragging rights—and scholarships. You have got to win, you just have to!!

It's the day of the big races. You can barely force down breakfast. The poached eggs taste like glue, the OJ is too thick, the toast is like cardboard. Last night you did the usual carbo load with fettuccine and butter and some cheese—lots of it. Sleep eluded you well into the night, or morning. Finally you were up at 5 am. You know it's not good to lose sleep. But there is nothing you can do now.

"Mom, I've gotto go," you say. She is driving you to the meet at the university track field; it's about 40 miles away. You barely talk, but you do remember your dad saying, "You'll do well. I know it. You're the best."

It's the first real compliment he's ever given you. It leaves you with both a warm an a sad feeling. You hope you are better with your own kids, if you ever have them.

Finally the hours of travel, suiting up, warming up, getting into the blocks are over. Every muscle strains, every molecule in your body listens for the crack of the starter's gun.

CRACK!

You push off the blocks with all your strength and hope merging into maximum effort.

Turn to page 132.

In the fall of your senior year, Gail is arrested for a serious car crash leading to the death of another student. It was clearly his fault. His blood and urine tested positive for significant levels of steroids.

Kids at school talked at length about "roidrage," the intense anger that is often a side-effect of steroid use. The anger and the aggressiveness come from high levels of testosterone in the blood, as well as stretching one's body beyond its normal limits by both growth hormones and steroids.

Some kids ignore it, saying it's a lot of hooey. Some are scared because they have taken some of the drugs not only for sports performance but to build muscle or lose weight or just be "cool."

Gail eventually is sentenced to 8 to 10 years in prison for vehicular homicide. Even Gail's well-connected father can't get the sentence reduced. It's a tough lesson for everybody. Death is permanent.

Linda and Samson meanwhile become like an aunt and uncle to you. They help you get a scholarship to the University and a continuing grant to do more research. You are on your way!

The End

From the very start of the race, everything is a blur! Everything. Time vanishes. The only thing you remember is crossing the finish line.

You win! You win by a big margin.

The crowd goes wild. People slap you on the back, grab your hand, hug you, scream at you.

Then you stand on the podium, medal around your neck. Nothing can detract from your sense of pride and accomplishment.

The nightmare begins. Your pre-race urine sample shows illegal performance-enhancing drugs—amphetamines.

How did this happen? When? You search for Devlin. He is talking to three officials; his face is cloud white. His arms and hands are flying about in protest. You hear his voice.

"Never! I never gave him anything illegal. Just a protein and glucose mix. You have to believe me!

But the tests don't lie. You are stripped of your medal. Disgrace hangs over you like dirty wash. Your career at high school on the track team is over.

Coach Devlin maintains that he gave you nothing illegal. You want to believe him; and part of you does. Maybe somebody else doctored your supplement or got amphetamines into your food. People who are desperate to win will do anything.

A dark thought crosses your mind. Maybe somebody wanted to take you down. Maybe they knew you were probably going to win, and they wanted to make sure that if you did you would be disqualified.

This is no longer kindergarten. You are in an adult world, like it or not.

The End

Despite how much you like Bud Devlin, his statement leaves you feeling kind of used. It's as if you were a work horse, his work horse, doing his bidding. You know that this may be unfair; after all, he has knocked himself out for you in so many ways. But you feel what you feel. It seems like what's important to him is his career, and you as a track star, not you as a person. Have you just made some bargain with the devil like in that old German myth about a guy called Faust? Faust made a deal with the devil to get what he wanted in life, but then the time was up and—.

Finally it's the day of the race. You are really pumped but also apprehensive. So much hangs on this one race. It's unreal and yet so real.

You feel good though, good and ready to run the race of your life.

Everything seems like a dream as you strip off the warm-ups and do final stretches, pump your legs up and down, take a drink of water—hydration is so important—and take in deep breaths. The sun seems brighter than ever, the air sweet, the crowd only a blur. The track is cindered with its white lines. You hear voices but you don't even try to listen to them—even Coach Devlin's final instructions don't really register. You are in the zone, that place where you and the moment become one, indivisible, unknowable, and yet all knowledge compressed into time and space.

Your feet find the starting blocks, your fingers stretch and splay on the red cinders. You are poised—time, stored energy, adrenaline, hope, and faith all bonded together. You are ready.

Turn to page 126.

Later that day you return to find Foster pacing the room in a state of high anxiety.

"Did you get it?" he asks.

"Yeah, here it is," you reply, handing over a letter from your mom actually signed by her. You feel dishonest because you didn't tell her the real truth about what you were about to do; but your mom has enough to worry about without you adding more. The letter she signed just references joining a research project on sports performance.

"Great. We're on. Gotta tell you though, Fox is suspicious of you. Seems that Gail is less of a friend of yours than you think. Gotta be super careful." Foster takes a practice swing with an imaginary golf club.

"So?" you reply.

"So, let's roll. They want to see you."

A mixture of fear and excitement surges through you. This isn't play-acting, this is the real world. Foster reminds you that your back will be covered 24/7. That is cold comfort when you think of Fox and his pig face, bulging muscles, and mile-wide mean streak. The guy is a killer.

As you make your way back to Gail's McMansion, you feel as if you're in a dream—or rather, a nightmare. Your awareness is heightened like never before. It is like the split seconds in a race when you seem to be truly out of your body, flying on natural endorphins and the super-consciousness that comes with maximum effort.

Turn to page 131.

You arrive at the door of Gail's house, hesitate before entering, and then walk into the hallway by the kitchen leading to the game room. It is unnaturally quiet, which gives you an ominous feeling.

The game room is empty. It's as if no one had been there earlier. The glasses and plates are gone, the sports magazines are neatly arranged on the coffee table. The giant screen plasma TV is silent. It is spooky.

What to do? you ask yourself. *Search for them? Just wait and see if they come back? Scram out of there and forget the whole thing?*

That's when the screams begin—horrifying screams and loud, angry shouts.

If you make tracks out of there right now and forget the whole mess, turn to page 111.

If you wait it out, hoping that Foster really does have your back covered, turn to page 114.

132

The double shots from the starter's gun signals a false start. Was it you? What a screw up if it was. Nope, it wasn't.

Back to the starting blocks. Adrenalin—the body's natural stimulant—flowing from the first false start. Concentrate. Give over to the moment.

CRACK!!

Go on to the next page.

Good start! Eight people with arms and legs pumping, pushing, straining, trying, hoping. 800 meters, two laps around the track demanding both sprinting and endurance. It's intense. You feel your breathing falter just a bit, you feel your legs burning, you see the runner next to you edge in toward you, you push as hard as you can, you feel power you didn't know you had surge through you, you cross the finish, the tape breaks and flutters in the breeze of eight athletes rushing past.

You keep on moving, partly from momentum, partly to bleed off the adrenaline, partly not daring to see if you won the race. Finally you slow to a walk and turn your head back to the finish line. Listen to the crowd roaring and shouting for the winner!

Is it you? YES!!!

The End

Check it out: Usain Bolt of Jamaica, gold medalist in the 2008 Olympics at Beijing in the 100 meter, 200 meter, and the 4 x 100 meter relay.

CREDITS

Illustrator: Wes Louie was born and raised in Los Angeles, where he grew up drawing. He attended Pasadena City College, where he made a lot of great friends and contacts, and then the Art Center. Wes majored in illustration, but also took classes in industrial design and entertainment. He has been working in the entertainment industry since 1998 in a variety of fields.

ABOUT THE AUTHOR

R. A. MONTGOMERY has hiked in the Himalayas, climbed mountains in Europe, scuba-dived in Central America, and worked in Africa. He lives in France in the winter, travels frequently to Asia, and calls Vermont home. Montgomery graduated from Williams College and attended graduate school at Yale University and NYU. His interests include macroeconomics, geopolitics, mythology, history, mystery novels, and music. He has two grown sons, a daughter-in-law, and two granddaughters. His wife, Shannon Gilligan, is an author and noted interactive game designer. Montgomery feels that the generation of people under 15 is the most important asset in our world.

Visit us online at CYOA.com for games and other fun stuff, or to write to R. A. Montgomery!